PRISONER OF
HOPE

PRISONER OF
HOPE

A STORY OF RECOVERY & REDEMPTION

ED COOK

AUGUSTUS INK BOOKS

Prisoner of Hope: A Story of Recovery & Redemption
by Ed Cook

AUGUSTUS INK BOOKS

Published by:
AUGUSTUS INK BOOKS
Woodinville, WA 98077
http://www.harmonpress.com/augustusinkbooks

Augustus Ink Books is an innovative imprint created to allow an author to publish her/his book in the way the author submitted it.

ISBN: 9781935959182

Library of Congress Control Number: 2011960704

Abbreviations used for other versions of the Bible:
AB *The Amplified Bible*
GNT *The Good News Translation*
NRSV *New Revised Standard Version*

Cover Design: Paul Staples (designhus www.designhus.biz)

To Carolyn, Sean, and Shannon

The people who loved me when
I was at my most unlovely

Love ya back

"I've been longing for Ed to write this story as only he can. Even though I already knew all the twists and turns the path would take, I loved reading it...living it, not so much."

Saint Carolyn, Loving wife
and partner on this journey called life.

Contents

| Prologue |
Why Tell This Story?

Nothing's as boring as a drunk trying to tell a story that he finds fascinating but has absolutely no appeal to a sober listener. Particularly since it's usually laced with slurred phrases like "No, wait," "I forgot to tell you...," and "Oh, what I meant to say was..." that make following the story difficult and understanding the point of the story—if, indeed, it even has a point—next to impossible. So, too, are the "drunk-a-logues"—long, rambling stories of adventures undertaken during prior drinking episodes—that sometimes dominate at a meeting of Alcoholics Anonymous. Examining one's life in excruciating detail may only be fascinating to the person who has lived it.

Why, then, am I bothering to tell the story of my own journey to recovery? There is, of course, the usual hope that my story—the sharing of my "experience, strength, and hope"[1]—will be of benefit to someone else who can identify with me and my journey and thereby find hope for their own recovery. The help provided to a person journeying in recovery through identification with the story of another is one reason why each edition of *Alcoholics Anonymous*—often referred to as The Big Book—provides several dozen members' stories at the back of the book. Our "own stories of hope…are our best medium to forging connections with our fellow human beings."[2] But the benefit of our stories is not simply to provide points of identification for others to connect their story to ours. Story telling transforms both the storyteller and the story hearer. "It is in telling our stories that we truly find ourselves."[3] When a person finds identification with the story of another, that person also finds him- or herself.

I offer my story not as a model to be copied in particulars, for it is my story. I offer it in the hope that it will model authenticity and openness. Authenticity and openness are the doorways to discovering the real, intended story of our lives. They are pathways to escape the false, constructed stories of our lives in order that we may discover what God may want to teach each of us through the living of our lives. If God is real, any interaction with him must occur in the realm of reality not in the realm of the false self we've constructed in response to the expectation of others in order to hide the fear that who we are is inadequate or unacceptable. To hear from God, we must learn to let our life speak[4] that it may tell us our stories.

So, I tell my story in hope that it will inspire you to explore and discover your own story and, thus, become free to be the self you are created to be. We often shy away from listening to our real story because of the pain of the process of coming to grips with reality. But behind the cliché of "No pain; no gain" lies the truth that for many if not most of us, we don't discover who we were meant to be without pain. Pain affects change in both a positive and negative way. We shirk from needed change because we hope to avoid the pain that will be experienced in the process of change. That pain is the enemy of change.

But there is a way in which pain can become the friend of change. When the pain of how we are living becomes too great, we either change or die. Pain can become the fuel on which the motivation to change runs. But to convert pain from an obstacle to change to something that fuels change requires reaching a point of desperation with life as it is— hitting bottom, if you will. The point was driven home to me in a talk with my A.A. sponsor. He said that recovery only starts with becoming free of our substance addiction. To move to sobriety characterized by serenity requires that we become free of the shortcomings and defects of character that enslave us to our false self. He said that the only change he would make to A.A.'s twelve steps, if it were in his power to do so, were two words in Step Six. Instead of the step reading that we became "entirely ready to have God remove all these defects of character,"[5] he suggested that change only happened when we became "*desperate enough* to have God remove [our] defects of character."

Someone once said that everyone is a theologian if by theology one simply means the explanation a person gives for the way things are as they interact with life as it happens to them. I have wound up taking an interest in and understanding of theology a bit further both through personal and professional interest. A basic approach that is being considered in Christian theology lately is called "narrative theology." One premise of narrative theology is that as we come to understand the stories contained in the Bible as being a portrayal of ancient persons' relationships with God, it helps us find, deepen, and better understand our own relationship with God. I contend that the same could be said for the faith stories of our contemporaries.

For those who may disagree with the premise that we are all theologians, perhaps the word "philosophers" could be substituted. The term that characterizes the development of

3

emerging Western philosophical thought over the last fifty years is Postmodernism. Leaving behind the question of what constitutes Postmodernism, let it suffice to say that in Postmodern thought the Western cultures are rediscovering the power of story, a power that more traditional cultures have never lost. These are all reasons for me telling this part of my story.

The Big Book says, "Our stories disclose in a general way what we were like, what happened, and what we are like now."[6] It's the "what we were like part" that often runs the risk of degenerating into a drunk-a-logue. "What we are like now" is a tale only to be hinted at here and more fully told at another time. In this book, I want to focus on a fifteen-month period that comprises the "what happened" part of my story because, since I've become a Christian, I've been puzzled by how often A.A. is looked down upon as a possible valid part of a believer's journey to faith.

Two incidents and a recurring conversation illustrate my point. I remember meeting almost thirty years ago with the head of a Christian Counseling Service that employed a dozen or so counselors. I had given a presentation on addiction and recovery to the staff of counselors who worked for him. The founder and head of the organization had not been present at the presentation. The counselors were excited and set up a meeting between their boss and me to bring him on board with what they saw as valuable information about incorporating twelve-step work into their counseling of alcoholics and other addicts. Rather than begin with my story, I began talking to the boss about the principles of recovery and their compatibility with the Christian faith. He interrupted me with the statement, "I've never met anyone with an A.A. background who was really a Christian." After a stunned pause I replied, "Until now." The conversation didn't go very well after that.

The second incident was an exchange I heard on a not-to-be-named Christian television network. A rather famous contemporary Christian musical artist was being interviewed. After some banter back and forth, the interviewer shifted gears. With a suddenly serious look on his face, he introduced the idea that the singer had "a deep, dark secret" with which he had struggled for years. The singer-songwriter-musician picked up the cue and began to talk about his alcoholism and drug addiction. He talked about how he had successfully hidden it from public knowledge but how eventually his personal life had begun a rapid plunge that almost destroyed his family and career.

The interviewer then asked him what had turned him around. He began to talk about going to "a Twelve Step Program." My ears perked up. I had often felt a silent disapproval from some Christians when I talked about my own recovery from addiction and the role Alcoholics Anonymous had played in it. Now here was a big time Christian star who, apparently, had shared my particular journey to sobriety. I felt a feeling of pride begin to stir in me as if him telling his story legitimated my own experience.

He didn't get very far, however, before the interviewer interrupted him by saying, "But then Jesus delivered you, didn't he?" The guest appeared taken back but said, "I guess so" and then continued talking about the impact of the program on his spiritual life. The conversation continued through several more interruptions about it really being Jesus who had delivered him from his sinful addiction as the celebrity tried to tell his story. The body language and vocal inflection were very telling as the interviewer became more stridently insistent and the interviewee's upbeat personality began to deflate before my eyes. Finally, the guest sighed and acquiesced. "Yeah, then Jesus delivered me." End of story. Change the subject.

About thirty years ago, my wife and I made the switch from attending one church to another. The church we were leaving had been wonderful to us and for us during the time we attended there. It had its strengths: wonderful people, strong children's and youth programs, good Bible teaching, works of charity and mission supported and participated in by the congregants, and support and encouragement for all of us to continually grow in Christian grace and character as followers of Jesus. The church we began attending had no quarrel with any of those attributes, but added to them a firm understanding that God continued to move in miraculous ways in the present day and an expectation that he would do so not only in the midst of our gatherings but also during our "everyday, ordinary life—[our] sleeping, eating, going-to-work, and walking-around life." (Ro 12.1 Mess)

As we began to fit into our new church surroundings and as people began to know me and my story, I seemed to have a recurring conversation with other members of the church movement of which I was becoming a part. When I would mention my addiction and recovery, they would wonder aloud why I hadn't just "prayed through to the victory" instead of going to A.A. I explained that when I went to A.A. I had no religious belief system and that, in fact, I considered myself an atheist. They were sure that I hadn't really been "delivered" from my addiction until I came to faith, specifically faith in Christ. I was puzzled by their reluctance to simply hear my story as I lived it rather than to have me edit it to conform to their preconceptions as to what a true religious conversion ought to be like. A person's assumptions and expectations have a way of making him or her unable to see other possibilities, particularly when those assumptions and expectations are derived from a religious position that he or she sees as unarguably right. As the saying goes, "None are so blind as those who will not see."

As my journey in faith has continued for the past thirty-four years, I am increasingly aware of the interaction of God with the humans of his creation in many diverse ways. Those in various communities of Christian faith find some of those ways are easier than others to recognize and accept as valid encounters with God. Admittedly, there haven't been many burning bushes reported lately or flash-of-light experiences occurring on the road to Damascus. But as the implications of a *missio Dei* (mission of God) theology are being worked out, Christians of many varieties are beginning to see the hand of God at work in many situations that are not religious and definitely occur outside of the usual settings of church meetings. The words of Jesus are still true: "My Father is always at his work to this very day, and I, too, am working." (Jn 5.17) The Father and Jesus find many more occasions to do their work in the 167 hours not spent in church each week rather than restricting their work to one hour per week in a church service.

As Jesus works the work of the Father in and through the Spirit, he is just as controversial now as he was then. He still refuses to conform to religious practices based on what the Pharisees called "the tradition of the elders" (Mt 15.2) but that Jesus called "the traditions of men." (Mk 7.8) The church of Jesus in the United States is just learning that the work of the Father is broader than what we might have formerly understood. The God who could use Balaam's donkey (Nu 22.21-31) to communicate with one of his prophets is not less creative now in using other non-religious and non-churchy means to achieve his ends.

The Christian Charismatic Renewal of the 1960s was a worldwide, trans-denominational resurgence of seeking and experiencing the Holy Spirit through various manifestations including divine healing. One of the mottos of that renewal that was carried over into the 1970s when I became reconnected with the church was "Don't put God in a box." We were told to expect the unexpected. It seemed in the years following my recovery and reconnection with faith and the Christian church that those who advocated letting God out of the box of traditionalism too often put God in a different box.

One of those boxes is the expectation many Evangelicals seem to have that a person's testimony of coming to faith must follow a well-known script. If I couldn't recall a specific place and time when I "asked Jesus to forgive my sins and come into my heart" so that I became "born again," my religious conversion was highly suspect. I wonder how many people have been ostracized away from fellowship in the faith and become "outsiders" because the "insiders" consider that they've not had an "approved" salvation experience.[7] I wonder how many people who eventually left church have heard the standard story of conversion so often and found that their experience didn't match it, that they have removed themselves from both fellowship and faith because they hadn't "gotten saved" in an Evangelically acceptable way. Sadly, the Evangelical church seems to be the poster child for a belief system characterized by the title of a book by J. B. Phillips: *Your God Is Too Small*.[8] Therefore, one of the reasons for telling my story is to broaden the perception of how some in the church think God is "permitted" to work in his ongoing mission of redemption, release, reconciliation, and renewal of a world whose inhabitants have been held captive to a sinful nature.

One final note. Some members of A.A. may be puzzled as to why I've chosen to use both my first and last names to designate authorship of a book that explicitly discusses my participation in a movement whose very name extols anonymity. To do so may be deemed to have violated the second part of A.A.'s eleventh tradition: "We need always maintain personal anonymity at the level of press, radio and films."[9] The "long form" of that tradition replaces the word "press" with the phrase "publicly printed."[10] I guess my name on the front of this book qualifies as "publicly printed."

Let me state that I do not take A.A.'s Twelve Traditions lightly. I think they are as important for maintaining the spirit under which A.A. developed as much as the Twelve Steps have brought over two million alcoholics to grateful sobriety. To change the traditions would be to change the program of recovery as much as to change the steps would.

However, we live in a different age from the 1930s when The Big Book was written and the 1940s when the traditions were formulated. In our age, rehab and recovery are readily acknowledged publicly by all manner of people of power, prestige, or celebrity. Repeated public references to "The Twelve Steps," "The Program," or "a recovery program" are now often made by those persons. One might say that the raised consciousness of the program and its acceptance by famous people has lowered the stigma of alcoholism and other addictions and thereby emboldened many not-so-famous people to enter recovery. This certainly seems to have been the case when former First Lady Betty Ford made a public announcement of entering recovery late in the 1970s—at least according to many statements made shortly after her death in July 2011 by those she had helped either directly or indirectly. On the other hand, many of the famous have simply used entering recovery as a "get out of jail free" card and then publicly relapsed and, perhaps, lowered the public's perception of the effectiveness and integrity of A.A.'s Twelve Step program of recovery. It's not my place to judge any of them or their motives.

I must confess to not knowing how these matters are viewed in the fellowship of Alcoholics Anonymous today.

After attending many meetings, almost daily for the first several years, I slowly reduced my meeting attendance until I was attending only one or two meetings per week by the end of my first decade of sobriety. My frequency of attendance might have continued at that level for years or decades until the present time. But in 1985, in my tenth year of continuous sobriety, I relocated to a rather inaccessible town over 1,200 miles from where I got sober and from where my A.A. base of support was located. The new location was over fifteen miles from the closest meeting, which resulted in me discontinuing attendance at A.A. meetings without having purposefully planned to do so. I occasionally still will attend a meeting, particularly if it's to accompany a reluctant newcomer.

Attendance at A.A. meetings has been less than sporadic for me for most of the past twenty-five years. Let me quickly add, however, that the Twelve Steps of A.A. and "practicing these principles in all [my] affairs" one day at a time are as necessary to me now to attain and preserve serenity in sobriety as they were thirty-five years ago when I had my last drink. I find "one day at a time" key to preserving both my sobriety and my faith. I've always liked the way that The Amplified Bible uses the clarifying phrase "daily delivered from sin's dominion" to explain what it means to be saved. (Ro 5.10 AB) As someone observed, the way in truly is the way on.

I don't know if members of A.A will consider the use of both my first and last names on this book to be an A.A. ethical lapse. If it is so considered, let me offer a sincere apology to any who are offended. I acknowledge that in A.A. "our common welfare should come first."[11] Please forgive me if my disclosure causes a sense of betrayal of A.A. unity. That is not my intention.

I pray that this possible breach of our tradition is not an evidence of pride on my part. As Tradition Eleven (long form) states, "there is never need to praise ourselves. ...We are to place principles before personalities ... [and] actually to practice a genuine humility."[12] Let me just say that it is not my own praise that I seek, but rather to give thanks and praise to the one who saved me not only from my addictions but also from all that would separate me from himself—God as I understand him. That is the God who was with me anonymously under the name "Higher Power" at the beginning of my journey in recovery. I now know him as the Triune God of the Christian faith: Father, Son, and Holy Spirit, made incarnate for us and our salvation in Jesus of Nazareth, the Christ of God.

Soli Deo Gloria!

(Glory be to God alone)

∞

| 1 |

To Be or Not

M y new life began the day I didn't kill myself. It was Wednesday, April 28, 1976. I had been out drinking the night before. That was nothing unusual. I had spent a lot of time drinking over the prior sixteen years, from age sixteen to thirty-two. Nowadays drinking at age sixteen isn't considered particularly young. But then, a slower pace of life that held the television sitcoms "Father Knows Best" and "Ozzie and Harriet" in high regard as typical middle-class American families with teenagers seemed to have kept my generation from experimenting with potential vices in late childhood and early teens—at least in the mid-America, middle-class, suburban neighborhoods in which I entered adolescence in the Eisenhower era of the 1950s. Those days are gone.

When I started drinking, we had moved from mid-America to Southern California on the scandalous, liberal, licentious, left coast. I didn't see drinking as a particularly rebellious act. At least rebellion wasn't my primary motivation. For me it was just a step closer to attaining the hip lifestyle to which I aspired. Much like sneaking smokes from age fourteen, drinking was to move me closer to the ideal hipster image. To be cool was to dress in suits with skinny-legged pants and to wear narrow ties and gig boots. Think *The Blues Brothers*. The smoke from a cigarette would curl elegantly around a poser's head. Some kind of intoxicating substance provoking an out-of-body buzz was required. It was part of the myth of the essential interconnectedness of Bohemian excess with an artistic temperament. Of course, as any teenage American male of the era could tell you, the pose would hopefully hide the image of adolescent angst, attitude, and acne, or, better yet, transform it into a *Rebel Without a Cause* indolence that would serve as a chick magnet. Didn't happen. But one could dream.

By that age I had discovered an identity in music. Not rock 'n' roll, as the rest of my generation had, but jazz. For me, the post-bebop West Coast Cool Jazz stream had caught my interest and defined my sense of what it meant to be hip. Later Charlie Parker, Dizzy Gillespie, Bud Powell, Thelonious Monk and the other East Coast Beboppers to which the West Coast Jazzers were reacting would capture my ear. But at that time Shorty Rogers, Gerry Mulligan, Shelley Mann, and Bill Evans had my attention. The Dave Brubeck Quartet was teaching us to swing in other than 3/4 and 4/4 time. Coffee shops like The Insomniac and clubs like The Lighthouse drew me to the scene. Having musical taste out of sync with the rest of my generation seemed to confirm my self-assessment as "different." I seemed always out of step with "normal," whatever that was.

Allen Ginsberg's *Howl* and Jack Kerouac's *On The Road* defined the ambience for a generation of counter-culture artists referred to as "beat." To be beat was to be hip, to be in the know, to understand at an esoteric level that qualified one as a hipster. Ginsberg laid out the quintessential image of the hipster in the opening stanza of *Howl*.

I saw the best minds of my generation destroyed by madness,
starving hysterical naked,
dragging themselves through the negro streets at dawn looking for an angry fix,
angelheaded hipsters burning for the ancient heavenly con-
nection to the starry dynamo in the machinery of night,
who poverty and tatters and hollow-eyed and high sat up
smoking in the supernatural darkness of cold-water
flats floating across the tops of cities contemplating
jazz...[1]

I thought to be an "angelheaded hipster" would be the height of cool. It was kind of hard being hip while living in a middle-class home in suburbia, but I tried as best I could or at least as much as I dared.

I wasn't up to trying heroin, which seemed to be the drug of choice of all the edgy musicians I admired. So, I drank. Whenever I could. Which wasn't all that often for a six-teen-year-old high school kid in San Diego's North County who was trying to learn to play sax well enough to survive the occasional gig. And, of course, to be cool. Alcohol was part of the rite of passage from nerd to hipster. So I drank. Even after a hemorrhaging duodenal ulcer caused me to lose enough blood that I had to be hospitalized, I drank. I would mix booze with buttermilk and drink. I reasoned that the buttermilk would coat my stomach lining and protect it from the alcohol doing any further damage to the ulcerated area. Inventive, but not very effective.

I was later to find out that I came from a long line of alco-holics on both sides of my family tree. My paternal grandfa-ther and my mother's only brother were both alcoholics. So if DNA and the gene pool have anything to do with alcoholic pre-disposition, I was a candidate to have trouble with booze.

There was always alcohol in our house, but I never saw problem drinking at home. The ten P.M. ritual was for

Mom, Dad, and Grandpa to gather around the kitchen table for a beer before bedtime—the proverbial nightcap. Occasionally, Grandpa would have his beer as a chaser while he sipped a shot of Southern Comfort. Sometimes Mom would join him and would have a shot too, but Dad never did. Dad was my stepfather and Grandpa was his stepfather, so their genes didn't figure in any alcoholic proclivities I might have. As for smoking, that was only indulged in by Grandpa. He was restricted to enjoying his daily half-dozen pipes-full of Half and Half smoking tobacco either in his room, outside, or during the nightcap ritual.

Leaving home at eighteen to go to college freed me from having to sneak around with smoking and drinking. Now I could find the crowd that displayed the image to which I aspired and simply act out to blend in. Being underage in 1962 really didn't slow down a burgeoning alcoholic. One could always find a roommate, friend, or fraternity brother to buy and supply.

The story of the next fourteen years isn't the point of this story. The pit of my alcoholism deepened, but I had always been a high-functioning drunk. I was part of an honors program in college and managed to graduate with a B+/A-average. I got married my junior year and we immediately had our first child. My wife, Carolyn,* figured that I was just a typical college boy who partied a lot and that when I graduated all this would change. Wrong. Carolyn was dismayed when I began to talk about enrolling in graduate school. She figured it was just a scheme for me to extend my lifestyle. She'd work. I'd go to school and drink. So she pulled some strings with the computer manufacturer's representatives she knew from the data processing department in which she worked and got me an interview to go to work

---

* Carolyn is my wife's name. All other names (except for those of my immediate family) have been changed to preserve their privacy.

for a major computer company. I did.

My alcoholism continued to progress for the first dozen years of our marriage. I learned to turn a deaf ear to Carolyn's recurring pleas to stop drinking. After all, I didn't have a problem. A tee shirt from back in the day stated my attitude: "I don't have a drinking problem. I drink. I get drunk. I fall down. It's not a problem." I made more money each year, worked my way through numerous promotions, and allowed the company to move my family cross-country twice to further my career. My success was proof to me that I didn't have a problem.

Most people at that time didn't understand that businesses have an unrecognized motivation to enable us high-functioning drunks to continue in our addiction. Most alcoholics live in guilt, shame, and fear. Feeling guilty for the social *faux pas* and family imbroglios we provoked, feeling shame for our inability to control ourselves, and living in fear that the whole house of cards we were trying to maintain would come tumbling down. Our guilt, shame, and fear drove us high-functioning drunks to overachieve in order to fend off any confrontation regarding our drinking. And as long as we overachieved and stayed out of trouble on the job, we could insolate ourselves from criticism from others and keep on drinking.

So, as I said, I had gone out drinking after work on April 27, 1976. I went out drinking after work almost every night—"just until the traffic cleared" enough on the Los Angeles freeways to make the commute home in a reasonable time. I reasoned that there was no point sitting in traffic while I could be sitting in a bar. At first it was just an hour at the bar. Then two hours. Over the years the instances of getting home 5 or 6 hours after work rather than two or three hours began to increase. Lately, I had even stayed out all night a few times. I had friends I could crash with. That's what happened that Tuesday night. With the bars closing at 2 A.M. and not looking forward to a confrontation by Carolyn when I arrived home, I drove 30 miles north to Hollywood rather than 40 miles south to Orange County. The unmarried friend I woke up (no wife to worry about there) wasn't thrilled, but he got ice, glasses, and gin and drank with me (he sipped, I gulped) until I passed out on his couch.

A few hours later, he rudely awakened me. He was off to work and I was off to...somewhere. I really wasn't feeling well. My arms and hands were burned where I had singed the hair off my arms with a cigarette lighter and put out cigarettes on the palm of my hand. I have no idea why I thought that was a good idea sometime between arriving at my friend's house and passing out. I was experiencing Durrell's classic description of a person with a hangover: "Mouth full of charred moths...sensation of having walked about all night on his eyeballs."[2]

As I headed south on the freeway I was faced with a decision. Option A was to phone in sick, go home, have the inevitable confrontation, and sleep until I felt better. Option B was to stop at a convenience store to buy shaving foam, a disposable razor, mouthwash, and deodorant and then to use a gas station restroom to "freshen up a bit" before going in to work, bluff my way through a short day, leave early by signing out for an imaginary destination, hitting a bar for a few drinks to "get straight," and then head home. The confrontation would be more bearable if I was anesthetized a bit. Option B was looking pretty good. I had done it before. It was doable again.

As I was driving south I began to play the "Tom Sawyer Funeral" game in my head. To refresh your memory, in *The Adventures of Tom Sawyer*, Tom and his pals Joe Harper and

Huckleberry Finn stay out overnight on an adventure that leaves them stranded on an island in the Mississippi River when their raft floats away. In the morning, they hear cannons being fired from a riverboat. In the late eighteenth century, folk wisdom propounded the belief that firing cannons over the water would cause drowned bodies to rise to the surface. The boys suddenly realize the townsfolk think they are dead. The thought excites them.

> Here was a gorgeous triumph; they were missed; they were mourned; hearts were breaking on their account; tears were being shed; accusing memories of unkindnesses to these poor lost lads were rising up, and unavailing regrets and remorse were being indulged: and best of all, the departed were the talk of the whole town, and the envy of all the boys, as far as this dazzling notoriety was concerned. This was fine.[3]

The outcome of the story was Tom, Joe, and Huck sneaking into their own funeral service and, at the height of the mourning, bursting out to reveal that they weren't dead after all.

The Tom Sawyer Funeral game was the name I later gave to the mental construct I would imagine when on my way home from a drinking bout. What would Carolyn think if I were to be found dead instead of showing up hours late either drunk or hung-over? Would the rage turn to grief? Would she wail and rail for me instead of at me? She'd be sorry then. What if my death wasn't accidental, but rather suicide? She'd *really* be sorry then. Would she see how she'd driven me to it, that it was all really her fault? Then self-pity would rise up in me. I would begin to grieve for my own imagined death and experience a sort of catharsis. I'd resolve to "shape up, knock it off, and do better." I would consider that my mental resolve should be sufficient to absolve me from the consequences of the current situation. Fat chance.

Here I am, speeding south on Interstate-5 in my little top-down Ferrari-red Italian sports car. I begin to play the familiar Tom Sawyer Funeral game. I had just gotten to the part where I was resolving to "shape up, knock it off, and do better." As I approached the four-level interchange where Interstates-5 and -10, US 101, and California 60 intersect, I thought, "You've got to get control of this. You're not getting any younger," I told myself.

Suddenly I had a jarring thought from out of the blue. This was it. Nothing would ever change. This would be the story of my life for as long as I lived. Immediately, I had an almost over-powering urge to die. I couldn't stand the thought of living this way any longer. It would be so easy to take the car off the top-level of the interchange and plunge fifty feet or so onto the lowest freeway below. Just a quick jerk of the wheel to the right and it would be over. My Tom Sawyer Funeral mental game had turned into an urgent desire to end it all. I was a split second away from a messy, grandiose, suicide—one that just might also harm numerous others on the freeway below. I wasn't thinking about the possibility of harming others, however. That thought was not in my mind and, therefore, did not act as a deterrent in any way. As so often happens in an alcoholic's personality, my only concern was for myself. As my hands tensed on the wheel to jerk it to the right I suddenly couldn't do it. Strangely, rather than relief, I felt like a failure at that moment.

I was pretty shaken. I did what any alcoholic would do. I found an exit ramp and drove to the nearest bar. East L.A.'s a rough part of town. I had no trouble finding a bar open even at that hour of the morning. Shaken, I stood at the empty bar, as far away from where the bartender was as the length of the bar would permit. I didn't want anyone close to me for idle chitchat. I needed to think. I gulped the first Bloody Mary and ordered a second to sip while I tried to sort things out. The second drink was rather quickly finished and the bartender brought me another without me ordering it. I guess my need and nature were readily apparent. Then I did something I had never done before. I put my money on the bar and walked away from a full drink sitting before me.

I had made two decisions. One, I was going to leave my wife and two kids. I'm not sure why that was my resolve. Maybe it was to avoid the turmoil that was bound to erupt when I arrived home. Maybe it was to distract Carolyn from focusing on my drinking by having to focus on what she and the kids were going to do. It's not that divorce had never been talked about between us. It was a pervasive threat that hung over our marriage. Looking back on that time, I think we both wanted to divorce—her to escape from the verbal and emotional abuse of an alcoholic relationship and me to escape the constant nagging about my drinking. It was just that we each wanted the other person to file for the divorce. I think Carolyn's motivation for putting the ball in my court was that the longer we stayed married the greater chance she hoped there was that something would finally change for the better. My motivation was self-servingly crass: If she was the one who filed for divorce, she would be the villain and I would be the victim. When my kids asked, "Why, Daddy?" I would remind them that it was she who had left me. They'd have to ask her. Deep down, I also knew that I didn't want the children whom I loved to think badly of me.

In contrast, the second decision was actually reasonable. I decided to call our family physician and ask him what to do about my drinking. When I reached his office by phone and asked for an appointment, his receptionist said that he was really busy that day. It would have to be a late appointment or possibly even tomorrow. When she asked me what the appointment was for and I replied that I needed to talk to someone about how to stop drinking, she said I should come in immediately. She'd make it work. It was several months later that I found she had struggled in an alcoholic marriage that ended with her divorcing her husband and that she was a faithful member of Al-Anon—a Twelve Step Group for those who are dysfunctionally co-dependent with an alcoholic.

The doctor saw me in an examining room. After a quick check of vitals and an abdominal kneading that I found out later was to check for size and hardness of the liver due to possible cirrhotic scaring, he brought me into his office. There he told me that my best choice would be to enter a chemical dependency rehabilitation program. There was one at the local hospital and he had already phoned to confirm there was a bed available. All I had to do was go home, pack a few things, and go check myself in.

I then phoned ahead to let Carolyn know the plan. I also told her that I didn't know if I'd be back when my hospital stay was over. I had no idea what I'd be like sober and how I would want to pursue living the rest of my life. My advice to her was to say goodbye as if it really were goodbye and we'd see what happened. I guess I thought I'd handle it all in one big event rather than have to face a second crisis when I left the hospital.

As it turned out, I didn't leave my family. Part of the hospital program included outpatient treatment for the whole family where we all began to understand and work on what was going on in the dynamic of our family system. We decided to try for healing rather than running away. But I'm the type of alcoholic whose fear and uncertainty are often masked by grandiose postures and idle threats. I wish I could say that sobriety instantly cured me of that character defect, but it's taken many years of consistent work to overcome that shortcoming. In fact, I must confess that in this area—as in so many others—the work is still ongoing.

My focus on what I wanted to do and on how I felt without regard to what Carolyn and the kids wanted or how they felt is typical of the narcissism often encountered in alcoholics. Such narcissists feel simultaneously both empty and invincible.[4] The emptiness inside promotes a sense of isolation and being alone in life. In that state, the narcissist has no regard for others because they are not even aware of others except as bit players in the movie of the narcissist's life. The sense of isolation and being alone is one of psychological pain, a pain against which alcoholics and other addicts self-medicate with their drug of choice.

The narcissist who self-medicates with mind-altering substances then has a diminished mental capacity to think clearly. That, coupled with the narcissist's feeling of invincibility, leads to risky behaviors that can be seen as self-destructive acts—the proverbial death wish, which can develop into suicidal thoughts. The feeling of invincibility leads the alcoholic to think that he or she can get away with the risky behavior without suffering the inevitable consequences. The feeling of invincibility is characteristic of adolescents, which makes sense when one considers that self-medication with mind-altering substances prevents emotional development. Alcoholics, therefore, are often characterized by lack of emotional maturity coupled with an addled thought processes. Such was the state that characterized me at this point in my alcoholic progression.

Addled thought processes do not serve a person well to understand what is happening at the time or to make plans for the future. Fortunately, I've subsequently been given over three decades to live, grow, and think back over my story from the perspective of more maturity and an accumulation of knowledge and understanding that can be found if a person is earnest about finding a good way to live this mystery called life. So the telling of my story will also include insights from these years of study and reflection on the experiences of living in and toward sobriety as well as in and toward faith. The thoughts to follow were often not contemplated during the period in which the instances I'm relating occurred. They came afterward. Some may think these thoughts interrupt the flow of story. Perhaps they do. But to tell the story without relating what I've learned from it as I've lived it, reflected upon it, and learned from it would only be telling half the story. As I've come to understand it, God impacted my story of recovery and redemption before I became aware of him or was even willing to consider his existence.

In retrospect, I see at least four God encounters on the day I didn't kill myself. First, I think the glimpse of a life devoid of hope was a revelation from God. A.A. calls such an experience "hitting bottom"—the end of the road, reaching the un-crossable line at which one turns around and begins the struggle toward a new life. Were I to use religious language, I think it would be called "coming under conviction" followed by "repentance." Conviction is the state of soul wherein one realizes that he or she is, in fact, responsible for most of his or her own misery. Conviction either leads to despair or prompts a person to repentance. Repentance is the realization that excuse-making and blame-shifting are defense mechanisms to protect a fragile ego. This realization is followed by a conscious decision to reject such defensiveness and to pursue a life of accepting responsibility for one's actions and purposing to live in a personally and socially constructive way. Conviction prompts the change and repentance is proved by the resulting change. Without change, there is no repentance.

Repentance is the often given translation for the Greek word *metanoía* found in the New Testament. The etymological roots of the word *metanoía* have to do with a change of direction or path. *Metanoía* is the noun form of the word group. Jesus' announcement of the Kingdom of God used a verb form from the word group to call people to change. Greek has a richness of verb forms that carry specific meanings that would be expressed in English by adding additional words or phrases. Because of this, the verb form of *metanoía* as used by Jesus to call people to repentance conveys a command for the hearer to initiate and actively persist in the on-going changing of one's mind about how one thinks of his or her participation in life as well as changing the direction of one's life.[5] The words "command," "initiate," and "actively persist" cannot be removed from the meaning of the call to repentance without stripping it of the intensity of Jesus' pronouncement. Repentance requires dedication. The Big Book says it this way: "Half measures availed us nothing."[6] Jesus said it this way: "No one who puts his hand to the plow and looks back is fit for service in the kingdom of God." (Lk 9.62)

Conviction leading to repentance can result in a person taking one of three approaches to change. The rugged individualist may embark on a self-improvement program. Because of his or her reliance on self, they go it alone. Seldom does that path lead to success.

A second option is self-help under the tutelage of a coach or group that will provide mutual accountability and mutual support. This approach may provide success. There is a power inherent in community efforts. The person realizes that they can't successfully maintain change on his or her own and uses a group of like-minded individuals to provide the external help needed. This is the approach of individuals who get sober using the A.A. group as their Higher Power.

The third approach is based on the underlying belief that all human endeavors eventually fail. For those taking this approach, help beyond human capacity is sought. This approach either actualizes latent religious belief or prompts one to consider religious options that have been formerly rejected.

I know from prior efforts that the self-reliant approach wouldn't work for me. I don't think I had ever promised to stop drinking entirely. I'm not sure if it was because I really didn't want to stop drinking or if it was because I knew subconsciously that I couldn't. What I had done with great frequency was to make commitments to cut down on my drinking. I invariably failed. Once I took a drink, all bets were off.

Self-reliance wasn't a viable option for me. I entered A.A. without religious belief so the religious option wasn't available to me either. Therefore, by the process of elimination, I tacitly undertook the group accountability and support approach. But, unbeknownst to me, I had actually, by choosing A.A. as my support group, set my feet on the third path. My journey to sobriety would ultimately lead me from conviction to repentance to conversion. Conviction created a desperation that provided me with the courage to leap into the unknown in hope that someone or something would be there to catch me. Initially, I was caught by something: the fellowship of Alcoholics Anonymous. Eventually, I realized that I had been caught by someone. I was on a path that would eventually lead me to understanding the Bible verse, "The eternal God is your refuge, and underneath are the everlasting arms." (Dt 33.27)

The second God encounter that day was in my inability to turn the steering wheel of my car to plunge from the four-level overpass. Some may think it was simply loss of nerve, but I think it was a physical check that stayed my hand for one brief instant, just long enough for the moment to pass when it would have been possible for me to swerve around the abutment of the guardrail.

The third God encounter that day was facilitated by the front office nurse at my doctor's office who interrupted a full schedule and squeezed me in because she knew how fragile resolve and follow-through can be in the moment of reaching out for help for alcoholism or other addictions. Years later, I undertook some training on how to facilitate interventions to gently coerce addicts into treatment. One approach we learned was called "take care of the cat." The idea is that alcoholics will grasp at any excuse to avoid committing to treatment. So, for example, if the person who is the subject of the intervention says, "I'd really like to go to rehab, but I don't have anyone to take care of my cat," the proper response is "I'll take care of the cat. Let's go." That day the nurse "took care of my cat" by getting me in immediately instead of postponing the appointment until later when my resolve to embark on a path of change might have weakened.

The fourth God encounter was in my doctor's response. My doctor responded with confidence to my request for help with a firm recommendation and referral to a rehab facility close by. That may not sound like a God intervention. It might sound like he was just doing his job in a capable, competent, professional manner. It was several months later that I had occasion to talk with him and thank him for firmly putting me on the path to recovery. He confessed that if I had contacted him a few days earlier, he wouldn't have had a clue as to what to do. This was in the early days of rehab centers. The one in the hospital to which I was admitted had opened only weeks before. Earlier in the week that I reached out to my doctor for help, he had received an announcement brochure that the hospital had sent to local physicians to acquaint them with their services and approach to treating addictions. He said that it was "fortuitous timing" that had placed that brochure in his hands at just the right time. I'm not big on fortuitous timing or coincidence. I think it was an intervention of God in my life on my journey to faith.

Albert Camus wrote an essay titled "The Myth of Sisyphus." The ancient Greek myth told of Sisyphus, who had been condemned by the gods to eternally push a boulder up a steep slope only to have it roll back down to the bottom when he had reached the top. The point was the futility of life.

Camus' existentialism had led him to conclude that life was absurd. He saw only one way out: suicide. He wrote that the taking of one's own life was the only action one could unilaterally choose. Therefore, each person had one and only one decision to make: whether or not to commit suicide. The choice not to kill oneself, however, meant that the person no longer had the right to complain about the on-going futility of being. If one rejected the choice to kill oneself, the only option thereafter was to continue on with whatever life brought. For Camus, that was meaninglessness, a condition that he and other existentialists referred to as "the absurd." For me, conviction—hitting bottom—had led to repentance—changing direction. I didn't know what was now to come, but strangely I felt hope. On April 28, 1976 I was presented with the decision to be or not to be. For reasons that I then could not understand, I had chosen to be. Something else other than the interminable cycle of drunkenness was possible. I didn't know what it was, but I was willing to give it a try.

∞

The Uncaring Agnostic

I wasn't in the hospital very long before God or some mysterious power orchestrated another one of the encounters that would prove to be instrumental first in my recovery and then in my conversion. It occurred during my first few days of hospitalization at the rehab center. The pastor of a local church came to visit me. That may seem strange since I was not a churchgoer. I knew Fred, though, not as the pastor of a church, but as the manager of an opposing Little League baseball team. My son and his son went to school together. And while they enjoyed each other's company enough to skateboard together, when it came to baseball they always wound up on different teams and thus, several times a year, I sat on one bench while Fred sat on the one in the opposing dugout.

He came to visit me because the night before he had seen Carolyn at our sons' ballgame but had noticed that I was not in my usual position in the corner of the dugout. After the game, he asked Carolyn where I was. She told him I was in the hospital, in the rehab ward.

So it was that during visiting hours the next day Fred had stuck his head in the door to my room and asked, "How's it going, Buddy?" To tell you the truth, I still wasn't feeling very well. My condition reminded me of an old Phil Harris' one-liner. In commenting on people who didn't drink, he said, "You mean they get up in the morning and know they're not going to feel any better for the rest of the day?" Detox and the first few days after in a rehab center are just not fun. My mouth was dry, my head hurt, and my body was full of unspecified aches and pains as sixteen years of accumulated toxins slowly worked their way out of my system. But I did the polite thing, and mumbled, "I'm doing OK."

Fred pulled a chair up next to the bed were I was sitting propped up trying to read a book—or at least holding a book in hope that it would discourage anyone who was passing down the hall from attempting conversation. But Fred had come on a mission and was not to be deterred. We spent a few minutes in idle chitchat as people do when they don't know what else to say. Fred offered a comment that I would hear many times over the next few months as more and more of the circle of my friends, acquaintances, and associates had their first conversation with me after I entered rehab. He said that he hadn't known that I had a drinking problem. He said he had never seen me drunk. To which I responded, "Actually, you've probably never seen me sober." The conversation lagged. After a few minutes it became apparent that he was about ready to go. Good. I was looking forward to returning to peace and quiet and hoping my post-detox discomfort would go away.

Then, out of the blue, he asked me if I was a person of faith. I replied that I was an uncaring agnostic. He said that he knew what an agnostic was, but he had never heard of an uncaring agnostic. I replied in what I am sure was the condescending tone of a bored lecturer explaining some arcane point for the umpteenth time to a dim-witted student who just didn't get it. "A Theist," I said, "believes there is a God. An Atheist believes there isn't a God. An agnostic says he doesn't know if there's a God. And an uncaring agnostic simply doesn't care if there's a God." "That's your problem, Ed," he said. "You don't care about anything." Without saying another word, Fred simply got up and left.

I sat there stunned. I was the one who ended conversations with caustic one-liners and then exited stage left. Who did he think he was, up-staging me?

I don't like to lose verbal jousts. So I sat there and seethed a bit. How dare he pronounce me an uncaring person? I cared about my family. Oh right, I had just walked out on them. Well, at least I cared about my kids. Oh wait, I was planning on using them in a manipulative ploy to shame Carolyn. I cared about my job. Or did I? I liked the approval I received when something I had done received public praise. I liked the "thrill of victory" feeling that came when something I had designed worked—particularly if there had been some expressed reservation on the part of others about my approach. But as for the job itself...? Like the bumper sticker says, "Work is the curse of the drinking class."

Normally when feeling bested, I would quickly move on to something else to salve the sting. But I was trapped. I wasn't going anywhere. There was nothing else to do at the moment. So I sat. And I thought. Not an easy thing to do when your brain's suffering from withdrawal. In counseling sessions I've often asked people to talk to me about a problem to which they haven't been able to figure out a solution on their own. Somehow, silent mental processes seem to race around old, familiar, non-productive paths faster and faster when we're stuck. By having people talk themselves through their thoughts out loud, it slows them—and their brain—down enough that the new idea that their racing mind had bypassed many times before could now be perceived and considered. Trying to think during withdrawal seemed to have the same effect on me.

I began to think. Was there anything I really cared about or was my life simply skating from one thing to the next, hoping to have a good time along the way, but somehow always disappointed in myself, others, or the experience itself?

I tried to think about what it meant to care. It seemed like a blank concept to me—a mystery to be contemplated like a Zen *koan*. About the only element I could establish that day was that "to care" would require me to have someone or something outside myself to care about. Caring focused on an "other" rather than on one's self.

Only later—much, much later—did I become aware that the recognition and prizing of otherness that was essential for caring was deeply rooted in faith systems. Martin Buber's *I and Thou* established that the "other" must be a "someone," not a "something." "Somethings" are treated with "I-It" rather than "I-Thou" relationships. "I-It" relationships are utilitarian. There is no mutuality. No "you scratch my back and I'll scratch yours." In "I-It" relationships, we use people for our own purposes as if they were things. "I-Thou" relationships, on the other hand, are always interpersonal. The ultimate example of interpersonal unity in "I-Thou" relationships is the unity of the divine essence within the Godhead of the Christian Trinity in a manner that maintains the identity of three persons without blurring the distinction or differentiation among them. According to Buber, the progression of "I-Thou" relationships eventually leads one inevitably to God.

The idea of an "other" also leads inevitably to God in another way. In Hebrew, the word translated "Holy" carries at its root the idea of the "other." The Holy is separate—other—either because it is totally transcendent or because it's been consecrated, i.e., set apart for another purpose. Therefore, that which is "Holy" is, by definition, something that is not me. I wonder if those who wrote the New Testament were on to something when they referred to those who followed the way of Jesus as saints—*hágios,* meaning "holy ones." They were "holy" because they were "other" than the rest of humanity. Their lack of the usual selfishness that the human race too often displays sets them apart. They were other than normal because of their care about and care for others.

Jesus embodied the concept of "the other" in his famous response to a teacher of the law's question regarding which was the most important law. Jesus answered, "Love the Lord your God with all your heart, mind, soul, and strength... and love your neighbor as yourself." (Lk 10.27) Clearly, my neighbor is an "other." One way to read "as yourself" is to paraphrase the idea behind Jesus' answer: "You know how you selfishly look out for your own interests? Why don't you begin looking out for your neighbor's interests with just as much enthusiasm?"

If the saints, the holy ones, were different from the rest of humanity in their ability to care, where did that ability come from? Was it implanted in them by being born by the Spirit from on high? (Jn 3.3) Did this new birth enable them to display the *imago Dei*—the image or likeness of God that is one of the attributes of all human beings (Ge 1.27)—in ways that can only be described as "otherly" or characterized by "otherliness"? Does someone require a new birth, an acquisition of the Spirit of God, in order to care at an intrinsic level? In fact, is it a characteristic of God's essential nature to care for others? Does a human being's attempt to care for others only become effective when that person is endowed with this essential characteristic of God's nature by the process of receiving the Spirit of God in some process called "birth from on high" or being "born again"?

All of the above thoughts about caring occurred over periods of time after I came to faith. That morning, sitting on my bed in the hospital, I had neither the language nor the discipline to think theologically about caring. But caring was what I thought about that morning. And those thoughts began a process that eventually would lead to deep theological reflection. That morning, as I thought about caring, I had more questions than answers. It's a long way from thinking about caring to actually starting to care. But as Chairman Mao remarked, "The journey of a thousand miles begins with but a single step." Little did I realize that opening myself to caring was also opening myself to God.

∞

Honesty

I remember the day I realized the importance of honesty in recovery. It happened in an outpatient group counseling session for newly recovering alcoholics and their families. We had begun some family counseling while I was still a patient at the recovery hospital. That beginning was traumatic to Carolyn in and of itself. During the first week I was hospitalized, she met with my primary counselor, Jack. She thought the meeting was for him to bring her up to date on my progress toward recovery. He did that within the bounds of what was appropriate while respecting patient confidentiality. He explained the twenty-eight day schedule of lectures and his counseling approach and goals. He also told her that family group therapy would be a part of the planned program. She was glad to hear that. Having been subjected to twelve years of the verbal and emotional abuse that often occurs in alcoholic relationships, she was eager for her and the kids to have a sympathetic ear as they tried to put the past behind them.

My counselor (and now hers) asked her what she was willing to do to facilitate recovery. Carolyn replied, magnanimously, that she would do anything to help me get sober. That's when the bombshell hit. Jack said that he was glad to hear that, but that he was asking her what she was willing to do to affect her own recovery. Boom. Carolyn either didn't hear or didn't comprehend his explanation as he tried to explain that families who stay in alcoholic relationships long-term become just as mentally, emotionally, and spiritually sick as the alcoholic and, therefore, need to participate in their own recovery process. What Carolyn heard was that somehow my drinking had been all her fault. I had pre-conditioned her to think that it was. Part of the emotional abuse I inflicted on Carolyn was my incessantly blaming her for all of our problems, including my excessive drinking, on the rare occasions when I was willing to admit that maybe I drank too much. If she had just been more understanding... If she had been willing to go out drinking with me I wouldn't have to sit in bars drinking alone... If she were smarter... If she were more socially adept so she wouldn't embarrass me... If she'd quit nagging me... If... If... If..., then I wouldn't drink so much. I drank because I was miserable and she's the one who made me miserable. Therefore, my drinking in ways of which she didn't approve was her fault. Or at least it seemed so in my mind. They say the best defense is a good offense and I was certainly offensive in both meanings of the word.

Carolyn cried at Jack's words, cried on the way home, and cried some more when she got home. Slowly, however, she began to understand what Jack had really said. He was for her. Not in the sense of being "on her side" as in choosing sides in an argument, but in the sense of wanting the best for her and being willing to help her toward that best. She had a friend and an advocate to help her make her life better if she was willing to accept the help that he offered. She decided she would.

So it was that a few weeks after my discharge, Carolyn, the kids, and I were sitting in an evening outpatient family group therapy session with three of my recently discharged fellow patients and their families. The scheduled hour-and-a-half was quickly passing with check-ins and suggestions to encourage progress when Jack began to focus on a family unit that consisted of a single Dad and his pre-teen son. They had been noticeably quiet that evening. Jack tried gently probing questions from several directions directed to the Dad and received a consistent stonewall: Nope, everything was just fine.

Meanwhile the body language of father and son was speaking volumes. At first, Dad leaned in aggressively with an ever-increasingly clenched jaw. Finally he decided he no longer wanted to play and leaned back defensively in his chair and crossed his arms across his chest as a clear indication that, as far as he was concerned, the conversation was over. During this time the son appeared first nervous and then somewhat frightened. He shrank back in his chair not knowing what to do with the experience of someone challenging his dad. Apparently, confrontation of the Dad—no matter how gently, lovingly, and respectfully it was done—was just not something that was done in that household. Father and son could almost have formed a tableau to represent the cardinal rules of the alcoholic family dynamic: Don't talk (about what's really going on), don't trust (the parents because you never know which of the Jekyll or Hyde personalities will show up*), and don't feel (because emotions are honest and the last thing you want is to become vulnerable by being honest in an alcoholic home).

---

* The plot line of *The Strange Case of Dr. Jekyll and Mr. Hyde* by Robert Louis Stevenson has worked its way into our cultural vocabulary. In the story, a good person drinks a chemical potion and turns into an evil monster. The plot takes on an allegorical dimension when one realizes that Stevenson struggled with excessive alcohol, hashish, cocaine, and opium use during his lifetime, leading him to foreswear their use as well as that of tobacco at various times. His wife noted the allegorical autobiographical dimension when he first read the story to her.

Jack turned his attention to the son and one could see a hint of panic flit across the boy's face. Jack's questions drew a series of "I dunno" responses. Finally, Jack turned to the group and invited us to participate. "What's going on here?" he asked. Awkward silence filled the space for several seconds. One could feel the presence of the discomfort that we all hoped would urge Jack to move on. But Jack wasn't taking the bait. He could outwait us. Finally, my eight-year-old daughter spoke up. "They're not telling the truth," she said. "They're lying." Out of the mouth of babes.

That incident began several days of concerted reflection on my part. I had been uncomfortable at Jack's probing questions. I had been uncomfortable with the silence that greeted his question to us as a group. I didn't want to talk about what was going on. I just wanted to bury it and move on. They say that the reason it's illegal to bury old tires in landfills is that something about the shape of the tire interacts with the subtle, constant shifting of the earth that covers decomposing garbage and—*voilà*—sooner or later the tire pops up through the surface. It's like that with our emotional issues and our mental mismanagement of reality. What we won't talk about, what we stuff back deep inside us, doesn't really go away. It just pops up again. And again. And again. Perhaps worse yet, we have to suffer alone whatever distress the issue causes.

One of the group exercises we had done in the hospital had each of us in our group take ten three-by-five cards. On each one we were to write a personal issue or memory of something that had caused us shame, guilt, or fear. When we had finished, we were told to arrange our ten cards in order from most distressing to least distressing and to place the pile of cards face-down in front of us with the most distressing card on the bottom. Then, Jack asked us to go around the circle with each one of us taking the top card, looking at it, and deciding whether we wanted to disclose it to the group. If we did, we turned it face up and read it to the group. If not, we simply put it back on the pile face down and the turn passed to the person on our right. We would keep going around the circle with the same procedure. Those who had decided not to reveal their card on the prior go-round were thus given another chance.

After ten rounds, each of us had a pile of cards facedown in front of us and a pile of cards facing up. Jack said that he and the group were now a resource to each of us to help us deal with the issues that were written on the cards in our face-up pile. He told us to pickup the pile of facedown cards and put them in our pocket. They were our private demons and we would get no help with them because we had chosen to keep them in the dark. As I've often heard it said in A.A. meetings, we're only as sick as our secrets.

The next night at an A.A. meeting a portion of Chapter 5 of The Big Book of *Alcoholics Anonymous* was read as usual at the start of the meeting. I heard the sentences of the opening paragraph as if for the first time:

> Rarely have we seen a person fail who has thoroughly followed our path. Those who do not recover are people who cannot or will not completely give themselves to this simple program, usually men and women who are constitutionally incapable of being honest with themselves. There are such unfortunates. They are not at fault; they seem to have been born that way. They are naturally incapable of grasping and developing a manner of living which demands rigorous honesty. There are those, too, who suffer from grave emotional and mental disorders, but many of them do recover if they have the capacity to be honest.[1]

I went home that night and underlined several phrases in my copy of The Big Book: "…incapable of being honest with themselves," "…a manner of living which demands rigorous honesty," and "…the capacity to be honest."

I was getting far enough along in the program of recovery to realize that Step Four of the Twelve Steps required that I make a "searching and fearless [i.e., honest] inventory of [myself]." That would be followed by Step Five when I "admitted to God, [myself], and another human being the exact nature of [my] wrongs." I was told that there were many ways to do a moral inventory, but that many people just found many ways not to do it. The Ten Commandments or The Seven Deadly Sins could be used as helps to prompt one's memory as the inventory was taken. The ambitious could undertake the Examine of St. Ignatius. Remembering the group exercise in rehab, I chose to list incidents that caused me to feel guilt, shame, or fear.

Now I had a problem. I had already confessed my wrongs to myself by putting them on the inventory. Picking another human being with whom to share them was no problem. That's what sponsors were for. I had two sponsors—a step sponsor, Wally, to help me "work the steps" and a spiritual sponsor, Clyde, to help me understand the "spiritual nature of the program." That would be a tough topic for me. At that time I considered myself an atheist. Any talk of God, religion, faith, or even spirituality was just so much mumbo-jumbo as far as I was concerned. I equated all of those concepts with "Dumbo's magic feather."

I had seen the Walt Disney animated feature *Dumbo* as a child. The story told of a baby circus elephant that is despised and rejected because of his huge ears. One night he gets drunk on champagne that had been accidentally spilled into a water bucket. He and his only friend, a mouse who rides around on the brim of his hat, wake up the next day in a tree. In trying to figure out how they got there, the mouse decides that Dumbo must have used his big ears as wings and flown them there. He is unable, however, to get Dumbo to risk trying to fly down from the tree. So he concocts a story about a "magic feather"—a feather he had surreptitiously plucked from the tail of a nearby bird. As long as Dumbo grasps the feather in his trunk, the mouse tells him, he will be able to fly.

Dumbo takes the feather, tries to fly, and does. When he later loses the feather during a flying exhibition in the circus, he initially panics until the mouse in his hat confesses that the magic feather had been a hoax used simply to get Dumbo to try to fly. Dumbo flaps his ears and soars away without his magic feather. To me, "God" was simply a type of "magic feather" to give people false courage to get them through things that they are actually capable of handling on their own.[**]

Not being ready to tackle the God question yet, I simply skipped the "admitted to God" part and sat down with Wally to unburden myself of my deep dark secrets. This was not going to be easy. I have always been reticent to share my innermost self with others. Since my inventory relied on my feelings of guilt, shame, and fear to prompt what I should list, to share my inventory would be like being the Wizard of Oz when the curtain hiding him was pulled back. Now others would know what I wished could remain hidden. My life was not the glittering image I tried to project. I would be exposed and susceptible to judgment and ridicule. I would be vulnerable to experiencing one of my private phobias: the terrifying fear of appearing foolish.

[**] The story serves as a helpful metaphor relative to understanding common triggers of alcoholic drinking as well. The protagonist is despised, teased, and ostracized, resulting in depression and feelings of low self-esteem or low self-image. Though accidental, it's the ingestion of alcohol that enables him to overcome his fear and rejection and let his real nature out. Sounds like the drunks I know. We may only be able to open up and let our hidden thoughts and emotions out when we're drinking. They come out, but unfortunately they come out under the influence of a chemical that suspends rational judgment and fuels emotional excess. Talk about a recipe for disaster.

Wally listened patiently and then asked me if I had admitted these faults without mental reservation to God and myself as I had to him. I started to say something about not believing in God. He interrupted me by saying that it didn't matter. If I didn't believe in God, then I should admit them to a God I didn't believe in. I told him that I wouldn't do that. That it sounded nuts. He then responded with a phrase I had heard from him before and would often hear again: "Then you just don't want to get well." He explained that I had to work the steps as written, not as I wish they had been written. He said that admitting my faults to God was a key component of setting me free from shame, guilt, and fear over my past. Wally was a retired Brooklyn longshoreman who at that time had been sober for twenty-one years. A wiser man than I would have thought that Wally just might know what he was talking about and followed his counsel. I figured that he just had hang-ups left over from his Catholic upbringing. Confession may be good for the soul (if there was such a thing), but I thought it was bad for the sanity of intelligent people to talk to someone who didn't exist.

Maybe something softened in Wally's heart when he saw how dejected I looked. He said that for now we could let the God thing slide and that I had written a good inventory as far as it went. When I asked him what he meant by "as far as it went," he said that I had just focused on my own actions that made me feel bad. What about all the things over which I felt resentment, bitterness, or self-righteousness—the wrongs that had been done to me that I still held against people? I should start a new inventory by listing all of these resentments and judgments and then carefully go through them one by one specifically looking at the situation from the other person's point of view. Where had I misjudged motives, unfairly blamed the other, or refused to admit my own share in creating the problem? Dang. This was going to be hard.

He also said that I needed to inventory positive attributes about myself and positive experiences and possessions I had. That would be the start of my gratitude list of things for which I needed to give God thanks. It was gratitude that would prevent me from taking "pride in one man over against another. For who makes you different from anyone else? What do you have that you did not receive? And if you did receive it, why do you boast as though you did not?" (1Co 4.6-7) When I complained about doing another inventory, Wally simply said to get used to it. Taking inventory would be a life-long process. Double dang.

This experience made me aware of a new dimension of honesty. What is sometimes called "emotional honesty" as contrasted to "cash register honesty". Cash register honesty is what keeps me from stealing. Emotional honesty causes me to examine my heart, which Jeremiah said "is deceitful above all things and beyond cure. Who can understand it?" (Je 17.9) But how much hope can I have if it is beyond cure? Why waste the time and effort if there's nothing that can be done about it and it is even beyond my understanding?

I think this is one of the reasons God said in the story of the Garden of Eden in Genesis that, "It is not good for the human to be alone." (Ge 2.18) We are designed by our creator to be social animals. We need help from others. As the Teacher of Ecclesiastes says:

> Two are better than one,
>> because they have a good return for their work:
> If one falls down,
>> his friend can help him up.
> But pity the person who falls
>> and has no one to help him up! (Ec 4.9-10)

Two—oneself and another—can often see together what one cannot see alone.

Jesus applied the same theme when he talked about removing the log in our own eye before we try to remove the speck of sawdust in another's eye. The log is our own self-interest and ego protection. It's there, but we can't see it. Someone else who loves us and cares about us has the disinterested perspective necessary to help us examine our own heart. Without the help of a loving community we have little chance of correcting our own faults. That was the point Jack brought home with his group exercise involving the ten three-by-five cards. Either I ask for help or I go it alone and good luck with that. If I could have dealt with the issue I would have done so already. Yet our broken selves seem perversely intent on acting out Einstein's definition of insanity: Taking the same course of action over and over and expecting different results.

I realized that this process of recovery would cause me to take a hard look at my excuse-making and blame-shifting. In my mind, nothing seemed ever to be my fault. I used people as verbal sparring partners. I sometimes described myself as a tap dancer—always on the move, cleverly shifting responsibility to others' shoulders, and escaping culpability. But as the wise writer of a fortune cookie I broke open many years later wrote: "Cleverness is useful for everything, but sufficient for nothing." I was going to have to quit the clever dodging and tap-dancing and begin to take responsibility for my actions and their consequences, not to the point of self-flagellation, of course. Everything wasn't my fault, but everything wasn't always someone else's fault either. I had played an active part in the creation of my dysfunctional life. Emotional honesty would require that I be willing to renounce my palliative self-delusion, look at my motivations and actions, and accept responsibility for the consequences that had occurred in my own life and in the lives of others.

M. Scott Peck describes people who are unwilling to live in emotional honesty as *People of the Lie*[2] in the title of one of his books. He says that the refusal to live with emotional honesty is the root of evil in a person. People of the lie deceive others by minimization, excuse-making, blame-shifting, and other forms of deceit that produce a life of uncertainly, confusion, and emotional abuse of those around them. They deceive themselves by refusing to examine their own lives with rigorous honesty. They refuse to accept responsibility for the harm they have caused to themselves and others. Renouncing my life of deceit in pursuit of emotional honesty would require that I be willing to accept a less than sterling self-image. It would mean climbing down from my self-erected pedestal. To do so would require humility. I wasn't very good at that either.

∞

| 4 |
Humility

I was having a bad day the day I had my first real taste of humility. After being discharged from the rehab center where I spent twenty-eight days learning the whys and wherefores of my addiction and a way to break free from my compulsion to drink, I requested a transfer from my employer to an office closer to my home.

When I entered the hospital, I was a manager of an operating unit in a branch office of a major computer sales and manufacturing company. The office was about thirty-five miles from my house. Los Angeles traffic made that over an hour commute each way. Having a few drinks after work while I waited for the freeway traffic to die down had been one of my standard excuses for not coming home right after I left the office. Part of the reason for my request for transfer was to remove the temptation to return to one of my "slippery places" from my daily schedule. A person has to form new habits to avoid relapsing into old ones. Another reason was that I was a fairly new manager at a branch office in the company. Learning a whole new skill set to meet a new set of job responsibilities was stressful. While stress itself doesn't cause drinking, inability to handle stress constructively often leads to the dysfunctional use of alcohol or other drugs to relieve the stress. So, I resigned my management position in L.A. to take a new assignment "back in the bullpen" at a branch of the company that was less than 5 miles from my house.

The route from my house to the office took me right past the hospital where I had entered rehab. Occasionally I would stop in on my way home from work. It gave me a chance to touch base with former counselors and to build some relationship with current patients who I would sometimes encounter at local A.A. meetings when they were past the tenth day of their hospitalization and were eligible to "ride the bus" of hospital-supplied transportation with other patients in their last weeks of treatment to begin an integration into the local A.A. community. A.A. works by one member helping another. It's not all altruistic, however. A basic principle of A.A. is that we enhance our chances to extend our own continuous sobriety when we help someone else. So I was showing up and beginning to work with others as a part of solidifying my own recovery.

I don't remember what made it a bad day. I just remember that by mid-afternoon on a day about four months into my recovery, I was climbing the walls at work. I was antsy, itchy, depressed, and angry at nothing and everything simultaneously. I knew that "relief was only a swallow away." I also knew that I didn't want to take that swallow. So I simply left work early and headed for home. As I passed the hospital, I decided to go in. Having some time with recovery professionals who knew me well might just be what I needed to come in off the ledge and stop my urge to drink.

When I got onto the rehab floor, I couldn't find any of my counselors. One was out sick, one was on maternity leave, and the rest were all busy doubling up on leading groups to cover for those who weren't there. The program director was away at a conference. I started to panic. One person who was in her office was Clair, the nursing supervisor. Clair was in recovery herself and while my contact with her had been limited during my stay mostly to my time in detox, I had always gotten along well with her. I liked her blunt approach and slightly off-kilter sense of humor.

I entered her office. After a few moments she looked up from the stack of paperwork on her desk with a "Yes, what do you want" look on her face. Undaunted, I launched into my tale of woe, looking for sympathy, reassurance, and encouragement that would snap me out of my funk, help me keep on keepin' on, and reassure me that things would get better. She gave me about thirty seconds of her time before she leapt up from behind her desk, grabbed me by my arm, and almost dragged me down the hall toward the detox rooms.

In case you haven't visited a detox ward recently, it is not a fun place to be. Detox is where everyone goes immediately after admission to the hospital rehab program I participated in. When I was in detox, there was only one other person there. The usual detox stay is three days. While there, the patient is given drugs to ease withdrawal. Contrary to popular opinion, some think detoxing from alcohol can be medically more dangerous than detoxing from heroin. If necessary, some anti-anxiety and anti-convulsing medications are continued after moving the patient from detox to the general patient population. Kent and I made it out of detox without incident. We were, after all, high-bottom, silk-sheet drunks.

Detox is also where some street drunks wind up. Like most institutions committed to rehab, the hospital I entered took overload patients from the police when the county detox unit was full. What greeted me when Clair pushed me into the detox room was apparently a street drunk who had been involved in some kind of altercation that had prompted the police to transport him first to the hospital's emergency room, then to county detox, and finally back to the hospital because county didn't have any beds available. His name was Ted, I found out later. The police officers had left Ted handcuffed to the hospital bed so that the staff didn't have to have him strapped down with restraints. His head was swathed in bandages, several with seeping bloodstains, as were several of his appendages that I could see protruding out from beneath the hospital bed sheet. There were other scrapes and bruises that hadn't been deemed worthy of a bandage, although I'm sure they had been swabbed and disinfected. Ted's left arm was in a newly applied cast from his wrist to above his elbow. When I entered the room he turned his head to see who was intruding upon his misery. He stared at me through bloodshot and jaundiced eyes that I'm not sure could actually focus on me. Clair pushed me toward the bed and said, "Tell him your problems. Maybe he has time to give you some sympathy." Then she quickly exited the room.

Ted and I stared at each other for what seemed several minutes of stunned silence. Then, having lost interest in what I'm sure he found a puzzling situation, he slowly turned his head back to its prior position and closed his eyes. I waited another minute or so and then slowly backed out of the room. I left the rehab floor but I didn't leave the hospital. I felt too shaken to drive, so I sat in the lobby to sort out my thoughts and feelings.

My usual response would have been to be angry with Clair for being an unsympathetic bitch. How could she, a medical professional and in recovery herself, no less, unceremoniously ignore me in my time of need? Anger wasn't what I was feeling, however. From the moment Ted stared at me through his pain I had an overwhelming sense of pity for him. I was stirred with compassion for someone who was obviously in much worse condition than I was. Actually, pity may be the wrong word. It was more like grief. I grieved that a fellow human being had to endure such abject misery. I grieved for the hopelessness I felt when I considered whether he would actually leave detox, enter the rehab program, and become a sober member of society. Street drunks had a habit of discharging themselves against medical advice as soon as they could leave after a seventy-two-hour involuntary hold. I grieved for Ted's family. Did they know where he was or had they lost contact with him? Did they grieve for him or had they managed to put him out of their minds? Grief turned to sorrow as I recognized the hopelessness I felt for him and the helplessness I felt as I tried to think if there was something I could or should have done while Ted and I stared at each other. And I sorrowed for myself as I suddenly realized how dead I had been emotionally throughout my alcoholic drinking. Sorrowing for yourself is different than self-pity. It's grieving for the years of life you've lost as you anesthetized your emotional pain with alcohol until all feeling was dead.

Actually, I did have some feelings while I was drinking, but they were distorted both in my perception of them and in the ways I gave expression to them through the impaired functioning of an alcohol-intoxicated brain. The most common emotions alcoholics experience during their drinking careers are hunger, anger, loneliness, and tiredness. Identifying these emotions as triggers to drinking led to the formulation of the acronym H.A.L.T. When a person in recovery feels hungry, angry, lonely, or tired, it's time to stop, get in touch with the emotion, and take corrective action lest the emotions lead one down the familiar path of dealing with them by not dealing with them but rather by drinking to dull them until they either can be borne or go away.

Anger and loneliness probably need no explanation, except for the strange phenomenon of feeling lonely in a crowded room while gregariously being the life of the party—a condition in which I had lived. But perhaps hunger and tiredness do require explanation since these words also refer to physical as well as emotional conditions.

The emotion "hunger" is not the physical sensation of needing something to eat, although physical hunger can be a trigger to drink. A synonym for emotional hunger might be "emptiness." It's an emptiness that we often sense as "yearning," a deep "longing" that emanates from the hollow core of our being. The emotion of hunger is a yearning or longing for a world that is not, maybe never was, and possibly never can be. A world where bad things don't happen to good people, where children don't suffer disability, and everything works out in the end and we all live happily ever after. It's a hunger for heaven or for a new heaven and a new earth where there is "no more death or mourning or crying or pain" (Re 21.4) and where no one does anything "shameful or deceitful." (Re 21.27) It's a hunger that's not just experienced by those who are religious. It's a hunger birthed deep in the human soul where we each intuitively know what should be and grieve because it is not so. It's a sweet sorrow experienced as we realize that we may never attain that for which we hunger. It's the hunger that drives our discontent with the nagging feeling that there's more to life than what we're living.

It's the hunger referred to in Bruce Springsteen's song, "Hungry Heart."[1] A hungry heart is what drives a person to leave home and family to escape a dead end existence—to try to find something better even if they can't define that "something better." A hungry heart causes a person to just go with the flow even if they don't know where they're going or what they're looking for. A hungry heart refuses to let a person rest until they get a life. Greg Boyd explains what's behind the hunger when he writes, "Everybody's trying to feel fully alive. Everybody craves Life."[2]

That kind of hunger would overtake me at least once a year for the last ten years or so of my drinking. I would watch Jerry Lewis' Labor Day Telethon that raised funds to fight muscular dystrophy. Yup, the whole thing. And I would drink and weep for "Jerry's kids," engulfed by sorrow.

Of course, I never contributed to the telethon. I simply used it for my selfish self-interest. The annual experience was somehow cathartic for me. Sometime during the night my sorrow for the children would be replaced by the sorrow of self-pity for the way my own life had been deprived of the one thing I felt I had needed most: my father's love during my infancy and early childhood. My biological father was killed in World War II when I was fifteen months old. I had no recollection of him. He was inducted into the armed forces two weeks after my birth. Except for those two weeks and a few days of leave before shipping overseas, he never had opportunity to hold me. So much for bonding.

My mother remarried when I was almost five. My stepfather loved me, provided for me, and encouraged me as best he could. If there's any fault for my deep feeling of having been deprived or denied what should have been mine by birthright, it lies within me, not him. Self-pity and sorrow would morph on those Labor Day weekends into anger for having been deprived of what should have been mine. I didn't know what might have been because I was never given the chance to actually know it. I felt cheated and was angry with myself for being angry at a situation that was no one's fault. For many years during the telethon that anger would erupt in destructive smashing of objects or punching holes in the walls or hollow-core doors of the house.

Tiredness as an emotion is emotional exhaustion. It is an all-consuming ennui in which one struggles to find the desire and strength to go on. It's the type of depression that often leads either to suicide or to recovery because the *status quo* simply can't be endured. It's the tiredness referred to in the phrase, "I'm sick and tired of being sick and tired."

But what does all this have to do with humility? My feelings of pity, sorrow, and grief for Ted completely removed me from the center of my universe. In the blink of an eye, I was no longer my primary concern. My attention had shifted to another. I had the unfamiliar sensation of caring for his wellbeing in that moment more than I cared about my own. I realized I was no longer an uncaring agnostic. I was still an agnostic, but in that moment, I cared about Ted.

It's not that I never thought about another person. It's that those thoughts were never exclusively about them but rather always deeply comingled with thoughts about myself. If I felt compassion for someone else, that feeling was coupled with feeling good about myself for being so compassionate. If I felt pride in the achievements of people who worked for me, I thought everyone else ought to express gratitude to me for having done such a fine job of training and directing them. In fact, I'd seethe with hidden anger if such gratitude weren't expressed toward me. When I was proud of my children, part of that pride was for myself, for what a good job of parenting I was doing.

That moment with Ted so many years ago jolted my world off of my self-centered axis and opened the door for me so see myself simply as one of many creatures on this earth. Not always to be excluded from the admiration or appreciation of others, but able to be admiring or appreciative of others when it was their turn on center stage. I no longer had to be the star of the show, but could become humbly grateful, admired and admiring, appreciated and appreciative. The second part of a prayer attributed to St. Francis started to make sense:

Grant that I may seek rather to comfort than to be
  comforted;
to understand, than to be understood;
to love, than to be loved.
For it is by self-forgetting that one finds.
It is by forgiving that one is forgiven.
It is by dying that one awakens to eternal life.[3]

I was a collegial member of the ensemble cast of this production called life. I was an essential participant in the company, but I was insufficient to carry the show alone. I could do my part and feel joy as others did theirs. I was feeling the first faint glimmers of humility.

∞

| 5 |
Willing To Try Again

Aportion of Chapter 5 of The Big Book was read at the start of the meetings I normally attended. The title of that chapter is "How It Works." At some time in A.A.'s history, an anonymous sage used the "how" in "How It Works" as an acronym for "Honesty, Open-mindedness, and Willingness to try what had worked for others." I think the "H" could just as well have stood for Humility. All of these are not characteristics or attitudes that I found easy to adopt. Like the bumper sticker says, "Those of you who think you know it all are pissing off those of us who do."

I thought of myself as being open-minded and willing in secular matters. One of my quips was, "I'll try anything twice." As a systems designer, I was always trying new things. Much of my enjoyment of college had simply come from learning new things. In fact, I remain a life-long learner. But regarding spiritual matters, I'm afraid I was much too closed-minded and unwilling at that stage of my life. I would have done well to heed an admonishment contained in The Big Book:

> There is a principle which [*sic*] is a bar against all information, which is proof against all arguments and which can not fail to keep a man in everlasting ignorance—that principle is contempt prior to investigation.[1]

I did, however, become willing to try one aspect of "what had worked for others" in regards to my search for an answer to the God question. I went back to church. It was on Reformation Sunday, October 31, 1976. But like many things in life, the action was preceded by a decision. The decision was reached a week before: Sunday, October 24, 1976.

I had been sober about six months. My life had settled into a routine that included eight to ten A.A. meetings per week. I went to a meeting each weekday and to more than one meeting a day most weekends. Whenever things got tense between Carolyn and me, particularly on Saturdays, I'd drop what I was doing and go to a meeting. I'd been known to go to three or four meetings on particularly stressful Saturdays. Sunday evenings, we'd often attend my second meeting of the day: a Sunday night open speaker's meeting. It seemed to be a time we could be together without bickering with each other. We were beginning to visit coffee shops after the meetings for "the meeting after the meeting" with a few new recovery friends—some of whom we had met through the hospital recovery program.

My regular first meeting each Sunday was a breakfast meeting held at a local community center. Breakfast at nine A.M.; meeting at ten. One of my sponsors, Wally, fancied himself one of the world's great pancake chefs. I don't know about that, but the pancakes and coffee were good even if the orange juice was canned and I always liked to spend time with Wally. In fact, I liked most of the folks I had met in A.A. One, however, could set my teeth on edge: Albert.

Albert had a high, nasal, whining voice that, coupled with several annoying habits, affected me like fingernails screeching across an old slate blackboard. It started with the way he would introduce himself before sharing in a meeting. We all basically said the same thing when called upon: "My name is _____ and I'm an alcoholic." Albert, however, would draw out the enunciation of his name interminably. "Hi. My name is Al-l-l-bert and I'm an al-l-l-coholic," he would whine. His second un-endearing characteristic was the repetition of what he shared at consecutive meetings. He would get on a jag and tell the same story or make the same observation almost *verbatim* at meeting after meeting until he finally grew tired of it, which was long after I had grown tired of it. In fact, for me, most of his stories and observations would have merited only one telling—if any.

Had I been a once or twice a week meeting attendee, Albert might have been bearable. We might not have attended the same meetings or at least I might have only heard a story two or at most three times as Albert seldom kept repeating himself in meetings for longer than two weeks. Then he would remain mercifully silent until he discovered another program gem to share with all of us for the next week or two. But I was going to eight to ten meetings a week. While Albert didn't attend quite so many, I probably saw him five or six time a week at the meetings we both attended. That meant I might hear Al-l-l-bert the al-l-l-coholic whine his way through the repetitious telling of a story in his whiney voice for upwards of a dozen times before he tired of telling it.

If you think I'm judging Albert too harshly, you're right. But six months of sobriety in the program had not yet developed much patience or kindness in my character. On this particular Sunday, Albert started a recitation I had heard at least a half-dozen times over the prior week and a half: "Hi. My name is Al-l-l-bert and I'm an al-l-l-coholic. You know the part of the Big Book that I like? It's on page 133 where it says that 'we are sure God wants us to be happy, joyous, and free.'" Boom! Suddenly, something exploded inside of me. No, it wasn't a rage in which I leapt to my feet and gleefully throttled Albert—although that urge had tempted me from time to time. It was a thought that was to change my life.

I had been in church all my life until I left home at age eighteen. I had quit believing in anything taught there by age thirteen or fourteen. But to live at home meant following the rules of the household, which included going to church on Sunday where we all sat three pews back on the Epistle Side (right hand side) of the sanctuary. After I left home, I only attended church when forced into it, either by the misfortune of being at my folks' house on a day when church attendance was traditional (even then I sometimes dug in my heels and said, "No") or when my wife persuaded me after much begging to visit my parents after each of our children had been born so that we could attend Mom and Dad's church to have the baby baptized. It didn't mean anything to me. In fact, it made me feel like a hypocrite. But it was important to Carolyn for some reason and some battles just aren't worth fighting.

The thought that entered my mind that Sunday morning after eating pancakes at my regular breakfast meeting was that in all my years of going to church I had never heard of a God who gave a rip about how I felt. My happiness was never the topic. How to make God happy was. Living in joy just wasn't the style of most German Lutherans, at least inside the church building and at church functions. At least that's the way it seemed to me. And freedom. How was one to feel free when countless rules, both spoken and unspoken, dictated the proper response to every situation in life? No, a God who cared about whether I was happy, joyous, and free was not on my grid.

Then the second thought came crashing into my brain. I had made a mistake. When my increasing mental development could no longer stretch enough to hold onto the childhood conception of God as I had come to picture him through years of Sunday School instruction, I foolishly threw the baby out with the bath water. I should have let go of the parts of my conception of God that I could no longer embrace and go in search of a God big enough for my new understanding. The problem is never that God is too small. It's that our conception of God often grows too small as we leave childhood. Instead of following Paul's advice to "put childish ways behind [us] (1Co 13.11)," we foolishly put God out of our lives. At least that is what I had done over twenty years before.

Though it hadn't yet registered, an apt description of my condition and mistake had been given in The Big Book of *Alcoholics Anonymous*.

> Some of us have been violently anti-religious. To others, the word "God" brought up a particular idea of Him with which someone had tried to impress them during childhood. Perhaps we rejected this particular conception because it seemed inadequate. With that rejection we imagined we had abandoned the God idea entirely.[2]

Then a strange thought entered my mind. It was not too late. I would not let my current atheism remain unchallenged. I was certainly still agnostic, but I was no longer an uncaring agnostic. I cared if there was a God because if there was one, I had better find him. Everyone around me said that my continued sobriety depended on grasping some conception of a power greater than myself to which I must surrender my will and my life. The Big Book of *Alcoholics Anonymous* clearly said, "There is One who has all power—that One is God." And then immediately added the exhortation, "May you find Him now!"[3]

That day I thought about how this God search was going to go. It seemed logical to me to look for him in the place where people reported that he hung out: church. So I decided to go to church the next Sunday even though I hadn't seen any sign of him there for at least the last half-dozen years of my childhood attendance. I thought that since my Little League coach friend, Fred, had paid me a visit when I went into rehab, I'd pay him a visit at the church of which he was the pastor.

Around mid-week I mentioned to Carolyn that I had decided to visit Fred's church on Sunday. Since she had often wanted to go to church in the past, I thought she'd be eager to join me. But she said that if I wanted to go, that was fine. But that she and the kids would stay home. Only later did I learn that Carolyn was afraid that this was just another setup. I would go to church, she thought, just to help take the heat off me and then slip back into my old ways. I knew nothing of this reasoning, however. So, Sunday morning, I donned suit and tie and headed over to see Fred and to see if I get a clue as to how to figure out this God thing.

I showed up, avoided anyone who looked like they were on the prowl to pounce upon visitors, and, avoiding an usher's urging to wear a stick-on nametag and to move closer to the front, sat in the back pew. Diligently reading the bulletin enabled me to avoid eye contact with anyone and provided the information that this was Reformation Sunday—an annual remembrance in Protestant churches of the Lutheran and Reformed traditions that was celebrated on the anniversary or the Sunday preceding the anniversary of the date of Martin Luther's letter to his Archbishop protesting the church's sale of indulgences: October 31, 1517. Later tradition assigned that date also to Luther's posting of his "Ninety-five Theses," which were a copy of the letter to the Archbishop, to the door of the castle church in Wittenberg. In 1976,

October thirty-first fell on a Sunday, so Reformation Sunday truly was an anniversary date that year. So there I sat, in a Presbyterian church about to celebrate the remembrance of an act that eventually launched the Lutheran church in which I had been raised.

I don't remember much about the opening of the service. But not very far into it, the choir filed from the choir loft at the right front of the chancel behind the organ consol and took their positions, filling the platform while a small orchestra filled the floor space at the front of the sanctuary. I would only learn months later that this particular church supplemented its choir with paid soloists and also invited guests from other churches to swell the ranks of their choir and hired an orchestra for some special occasions. This was to be one of them.

The bulletin had announced the performance of "Variations on 'A Mighty Fortress Is Our God,' arranged for choir and orchestra." How appropriate. "A Mighty Fortress" was composed by Martin Luther (to the tune of a traditional tavern beer-drinking song, I might add) and served as the battle hymn of the Reformation. Not knowing what to expect, I felt a chill run through my body as the orchestra started with a tympani roll and a *tutti* section with all instruments *fortissimo*, the organ came to life with all stops engaged, and the choir joining in full voice. Wow! The sound was magnificent.

I felt a swelling begin in my chest and a lump forming in my throat. As a musician, I had played various "Theme and Variation" pieces both on the piano and as part of a concert band. The usual arc of such arrangements is to start with a simple statement of the theme and then proceed through several variations, each one more complex, until the piece finishes with a thrilling climax of musical complexity. This arrangement was just the opposite. After a thunderous opening statement of the hymn's theme full of baroque embellishments, each variation was simplified until the second to the last variation was simply four-part hymnody with chamber music accompaniment. For the "climax," if you will, the orchestra and organ remained silent while the choir simply sang the opening stanza of the hymn in unison, *a capella*. Such power. Simple human voices, full of trust and confidence, singing to their God without benefit of artifice, ornamentation, or accompaniment. I was enthralled. I was undone. I was in tears. I didn't know what had just happened, but I knew something had. Somehow, on shaky legs, I left the church and drove home.

So that's how I went back to church. On Reformation Sunday, 1976. Reformation Sunday being a remembrance of the sixteenth-century Reformation that had brought the "Five *solas*" to the center of what became known as Protestant Reformed theology:

1. *Sola scriptura*—by Scripture alone

2. *Sola fide*—by faith alone

3. *Sola gratia*—by grace alone

4. *Solo Christo*—through Christ alone, and

5. *Soli Deo Gloria*—glory to God alone

I didn't know what I thought about Scripture—the Bible. After all, it contained stories of a flood that killed everyone on earth except for Noah and his family who survived in an Ark that had held two of every living thing, Jonah living three days in the belly of a great fish, three Hebrew children living through an ordeal in a fiery furnace, not to mention someone rising from the dead. Those stories and others had seriously challenged my belief system over twenty years ago. *Sola scriptura* had a few hurdles to overcome.

I had no faith so if something were to happen it would have to be by grace alone.

Solo Christo seemed terribly narrow-minded. What of the billions of people who had never heard of Jesus? Would they just be flicked into the flaming eternity of hell like the ash from the tip of God's cigarette?

As for "glory to God alone," there was God, again, hogging the spotlight. I was interested in finding out about a God who cared about me being happy, joyous, and free. I had lost interest in a God who was an eternal egomaniac who demanded my conformity to his rules in order for him to be happy.

Obviously, though, some sort of beginning had been made. I knew my emotions had been stirred but I also felt that it was more than just emotions. A step had been taken, but the path ahead was far from clear. Like they say in A.A., "More will be revealed." I certainly needed more to answer my Higher Power question than one experience on a Sunday morning, no matter how moving it had been.

∞

Commitment

I remember the day I committed to my marriage. No, I don't mean the day of the wedding with its "till death do us part" and all that. Frankly, our wedding wasn't much of an affair. Carolyn and I found ourselves pregnant about four months into our relationship. By "found ourselves" I don't mean we didn't know how it happened. Even we were smart enough to figure that out. What I mean by "found ourselves" is that my adolescent sense of invulnerability didn't work very well as a birth control method. We were still in the age bracket where, in our own minds, nothing bad was ever going to happen to us. Other people, yes, but not to us. We were both twenty. I keep saying "we," but in all fairness, I need to speak for myself. Each person has their own story and it's their prerogative not only how to tell it but also whether to tell it. It's where our stories intersect those of someone else that one person's choice of if and how to tell his or her story may impinge on the rights of the other person to make his or her own choice regarding disclosure. So, it is with some trepidation that I may trammel or usurp Carolyn's rights that I tell my view of our intertwined stories.

Intellectually I knew that bad things could happen to anyone and that being me wasn't an impenetrable barrier to "the heart-ache, and the thousand natural shocks that flesh is heir to."[1] But much as we like to think ourselves rational beings, more decisions are made in the gut than in the head. Like many, if not most, twenty year-olds, I believed myself to be invincible, a legend in my own mind.

The debate began. I wasn't ready to be married and a parent. I was about to begin my junior year in college. I thought I had the perfect solution: Carolyn would get an abortion. The time was almost ten years before the Supreme Court's Roe v. Wade decision would make abortion a legal option and establish abortion decisions as the woman's choice. So my "perfect solution" would involve an illegal activity in which I would not be the person at risk and making a choice that the law would later say was not mine to make. The "perfect solution" was indicative of the self-centered focus of my life, not only in that period but also in the whole of my life up to that time and for more than a dozen years to follow.

Carolyn was adamant that she was not going to have an abortion. I didn't know her well then. We had only known each other for five months or so. I was seeing the root of what I would come to discover was her deep and profound respect for life. It was a respect grounded in awe. For Carolyn, children—especially up to the age of three or four—are profound wonders. The unfolding of curiosity, speech, and locomotion never cease to amaze her. Nor is her fascination with life limited to lives emerging into personhood. Carolyn and I provided a home and Carolyn provided care for her aging mother for several years until she could no longer provide the needed care for her. Then her mother was admitted to a "nursing home" or whatever the currently acceptable euphemism is now for what was once called an "old folks home." Carolyn would visit her daily. Each visit revealed continued neglect of some basic care element that could appropriately be described as elder abuse. The "home" was basically a warehouse for geriatrics. Carolyn became her Mom's advocate, demanding better care for her mother. She also tried to ameliorate the effects of neglect to other patients by learning their names and extending simple kindnesses to them. Finally a bed opened up at a really good facility even nearer to our house and Carolyn was able to get her Mom admitted to that facility.

The quality of care there relieved Carolyn of the sense of obligation to visit daily to advocate for her mother. In fact, the staff suggested that Carolyn's daily visits worked against her mom establishing friendships with other residents there. So Carolyn limited herself to four or five visits a week at random times on random days. Carolyn continued her practice at that new facility of learning names, needs, and likes and dislikes of the residents. She befriended the nurses and leant a helping hand when other urgencies prevented them from responding quickly to patients with less urgent needs. Carolyn's awe of early development stages of life and genuine respect and loving care for the elderly has become a focus of my deep and profound admiration of her. I didn't know then that this was possibly behind her refusal to even consider an abortion. But I did know, in no uncertain terms, that she was not going to have one.

I knew what Carolyn wasn't going to do, but I didn't know what I was going to do. Then I had an attack of scruples. I would marry her. Not because I thought there was anything scurrilous or scandalous about children born out of wedlock, but because of the specter of a fatherless child. I had been one after the death of my father during World War II when I was fifteen months old. My mother's remarriage just before my fifth birthday provided me with a stepfather. Stepfathers, like fathers, can be good, bad, or indifferent. Or maybe there is no such thing as "indifferent" if indifference is equated with neglect and neglect is tacit abuse by ignoring the value of the child. My stepfather was no different than most "good" fathers. He had his faults as well as his virtues, but he never failed to treat me as one of his own. Maybe I would have felt less "fatherless" if he had adopted me. But doing so would have meant forfeiting the benefits to which I was entitled as the sole surviving son of a person killed on active duty in the military. That was not a decision to be made lightly because my adoption would have resulted in me forfeiting the right to go to college on my father's G.I. Bill. No, the lack of feeling a secure paternal relationship lay with me, not with him. For some reason, I had always felt like an outsider. As I grew old enough to put words to the feeling and to wonder at its source, I came to believe that it was rooted in my lack of paternal bonding at a young age—what some have called a "father wound." I was not going to subject a child to that possibility.

So it was more out of an ethical consideration for the possible future sense of wellbeing of an unborn child than for any deep love for Carolyn that I proposed marriage as the way out of our dilemma. When I speak of a lack of deep love for Carolyn, I don't mean that I didn't like her. After all, she was my girlfriend. But five months' acquaintanceship and even less of relationship is no basis on which to choose life partners. Particularly when the people making the decision are twenty years old and faced with the problem of an unwanted pregnancy.

Fortunately, over time, love did come into our marriage. It was somewhat like the process described in a song in *Fiddler on the Roof*.[2] The characters Tevye and Golde were married through an arranged marriage twenty-five years earlier. The duet "Do You Love Me?" relates their pre-nuptial concern that they're not in love. Their parents tell them not to worry and assure them that they'll learn to love one another. The song poignantly conveys Tevye's question twenty-five years into the marriage as to whether Golde has come to love him. Golde replies with a long litany of the day-to-day tasks that have filled their life together for a quarter of a century. Tevye hazards a conclusion on her behalf: I guess you love me. When Golde accedes, Tevye concludes that he must love her too. That's a bit how it was with Carolyn and me. After forty-seven years of marriage, I am happy to report that I do love my wife and I have reason to suppose she loves me too.

Being twenty years old and being residents of California brought another complication. At that time, 1964, we would each have needed parental consent to marry because we were both under the age of twenty-one. I don't know how Carolyn felt about discussing the matter with her parents. She had lived on her own for several years. But I know exactly how I felt about discussing it with my parents. It wasn't going to happen. Even then I lived a life motto that said "It's easier to ask for forgiveness than it is for permission." Fortunately, we were a short, six-hour drive from Las Vegas where eighteen was the legal age to marry and a valid driver's license was sufficient identification to obtain a marriage license. Since there was no waiting period in Clark County Nevada, the happy couple could obtain a marriage license and immediately step across the hall to a county clerk's office and solemnize the union. And so we did on November 7, 1964, three weeks after my twenty-first birthday.

The marriage wasn't off to an auspicious start. I took Carolyn back to the motel room we shared with the cockroaches. I kissed her goodnight and went out to party the rest of the night. I'm not much of a gambler, but gambling meant free drinks. So I nursed my bets and gulped my drinks at a crowded crap table where it was easy to stay out of the betting for extended periods of time. But I would be at the table when the drink girl came by with the ubiquitous question, "Cocktails?" and thereby be eligible to drink at the house's expense. The trick was finding where the $2 tables were. I would stay at one until the dealers started giving me that look that indicated they wondered when I would get around to making a bet. Then I'd make a bet or two and sit out a number of rolls and have another drink. After a while I'd move to another $2 table and start the procedure again. Follow the crowd. Stay in the flow. Gulp your drinks and parsimoniously dole out your bets. I gave a whole new meaning to the term "cheap drunk."

Sunday morning brought a hangover, some "hair of the dog," and the prospect of a six-hour drive home. Less than halfway there, with the car laboring up a long grade to Halloran Summit, we blew the engine of my '54 Ford. We had $13 left between us. The car was towed to the closest garage and deemed by me to be not worth fixing. The owner of the garage suggested that I sign over the title to the car to cover the tow charge. That sounded like a good solution to me. I would do it. That is, I would if I could. Technically, it wasn't my car. My folks had retained title to help give me a financial break on my insurance by keeping the car on their policy. I had paid them for the car and regularly paid them for the insurance premium, but they would have to dispose of the car. The owner of the garage agreed that I could leave the car there for a time while I worked out either my folks' signatures on the title, raise the money for the tow and repairs, or pay for the tow and remove it from the lot somehow. I was going to need a clear head and some time to figure out how to have this conversation with my folks. Someone at the garage was headed toward Los Angeles and agreed to drop us off at Carolyn's apartment in Orange County for $10 gas money. That left us with $3. We headed for home. Some honeymoon.

A few days later, I called the folks. I decided to lead with the news that Carolyn and I had eloped, hoping that it would be taken as some kind of good news and then I could slip in the fact that the car was demolished as an "Oh, by the way." I survived the conversation. But it was not of the type that I wanted to have again any time soon. Dad decided to rent a tow bar, drive to Halloran Summit the next weekend, pay the towing and storage fees, and tow the car back home. On the way home, he rolled the car. He severely gashed the fingers on the hand that was thrust out the driver's side window. I could have told him that the prospects for a successful venture coming out of anything even remotely connected to the trip of the prior weekend were someplace between slim and none. But he didn't ask my opinion and wouldn't have heeded it even if I had offered it.

And so began our alcoholic marriage. It was neither fun nor pretty. I lived with a huge resentment. In my warped alcoholic thinking, full of narcissism and self-pity, I had given up my plans for life to do the right thing and bail Carolyn out of a mess. The fact that I really didn't have any particular plans for life at that time was immaterial as far as I was concerned. If I had had them, I'd have had to give them up, and now it made no sense to formulate any plans for the future based on my wants because I was trapped. At least that's how my alcoholic logic saw the situation. Self-pity and resentment foment anger, so I was a very angry person. That anger came out in abusive behavior. I was never physically abusive. I never hit or even shoved Carolyn, but my attitude and physical aspect made me threatening and intimidating at times. Yelling, sarcasm, and other forms of verbal abuse became my normal interaction with Carolyn.

Years later, after I got sober, I saw a Billy Crystal movie that brought it home to me. Billy played an aging entertainer who had worked his way up from vaudeville, through clubs and resorts doing lounge act standup *schtick*, first to the main rooms and then, finally, to being a television star in the 1950s. In the film, he acquired a nickname that served as the title of the movie—*Mr. Saturday Night*. Beside him through all the years was his behind-the-scenes older brother serving tirelessly as valet, agent, manager, accountant, travel coordinator—whatever Billy's character needed.

Toward the end of the movie, Mr. Saturday Night, in his seventies, is now definitely past the peak of his career. Though not yet at its lowest point, the handwriting's on the wall and everyone but Billy can see it. So his older brother, approaching his eighties, tells Billy he's quitting. He and his long-standing, long-suffering wife have put away a little money over the years and bought a house in the Florida sunshine. He's ready to come in off the road and retire. Billy is irate. Screaming, "You ingrate! What did I ever do to you?" he begins to pummel his brother. For a few moments the two old men ineffectually slap at each other— Billy on the attack and his brother simply trying to defend himself. They stumble across the dressing room and down a short flight of stairs to a landing where they both finally disengage, panting and disheveled.

Billy starts up again morosely, this time in a shame-inducing whine full of hurt emotion. "What did I do that was so terrible? Who gave you a job when no one would have you? Who put food on your table? Who went without to give you money for your kid to go to college? Who gave, and gave, and gave? And this is the thanks I get? What did I do to you that was so terrible?" His brother simply looks at him with an expression weighed down by over sixty years of unrecognized and unappreciated devotion and simply says, "You could have been nicer."

That's the story of my alcoholic marriage. I could have been nicer. I was nasty without provocation, ever ready to take offense and pick a fight. Someone had to pay for what I suffered by way of self-pity, resentment, and anger. I decided it was Carolyn. I could always find a way to blame her for everything and anything. Nothing was my fault. It was all her fault. Rules may apply to others. But I was different. Years later a friend would say to me, "You're problem is that you think that every sign you see ("No U-turn," Keep Off the Grass," "Do Not Touch," etc.) has fine print at the bottom that says, 'Except for Ed.'" I was me, one of a kind, unique. I'm lucky I didn't die of terminal uniqueness.

I now know it was irrational, but that's the way drunks think—at least that's the way this drunk thought. It was a manifestation of the evil of avoiding responsibility at any cost that I wrote about in Chapter 3, the chapter on honesty. It was evil. I was evil. But it was my pattern. To this day Carolyn and I still joke about it with gallows humor. When something goes wrong, she'll say, "I guess that's my fault too." I'll reply, "Of course. I don't know how or why yet, but I'll think of something." We don't really laugh at those exchanges. They serve as reminders as to how sick I was and how sick she was to put up with my attitudes and actions. A commonly heard quote says, "Those who cannot remember the past are condemned to repeat it."[3] So we remember, acknowledge the remembered dysfunction, and silently vow not to return to it. I could have been nicer.

If there's an upside to this period of dysfunctional marriage it's this: no matter how grim the tale others tell Carolyn and me of their relational woes, we don't give up on them. We know from where we've come and that the painful process of change can be survived until the miracle happens. Therefore, we never consider anyone hopeless. If they can't find hope in our story we simply ask them to let us have hope for them until they can have hope for themselves.

Then there were the kids. As nasty as I was to Carolyn, I tried hard to be a good father. I really loved those kids. Still do, as a matter of fact. I can remember with embarrassment occasions when my pattern of yelling, blaming, belittling, and venting my anger spilled over onto the kids as a form of intimidation toward getting my own way. My emotional on-off switch wasn't working as well as it once did. I can still remember the hurt in my children's eyes when I think of some of these low points.

I'd learn later in A.A. about making amends and tried to do so to Carolyn and the kids. But words that wound really can't be taken back. My sponsor said that we needed to make amends to the people closest to us for the rest of our lives. An amends begins with words, but the real amends is living a lifetime in a transformed and ever-improving relationship with those we've hurt most, which are, ironically, usually those we love most. It doesn't happen over night. But what else are we going to do with the rest of our life except try to learn to be nicer; especially to those we love most?

One may wonder why we continued to stay together. One reason was that Carolyn did think I was a good father. To divorce would have caused our kids to pay the price of my alcoholic and Carolyn's co-dependent marriage. Of course, they already were paying a price. It's unavoidable. Dysfunction produces pain and one way to cope with the pain is to develop one's own dysfunctional defense mechanisms. Children in alcoholic homes learn the basic rules of survival: Don't talk, Don't Trust, Don't Feel. The developmental problems associated with children raised in alcoholic homes even caused a recovery program to be devised for them: Adult Children of Alcoholics.

One sick reason I stayed married to Carolyn was simply because she didn't divorce me. We had spoken of divorce numerous times through those first twelve years. I would urge her to do it. I told her I'd be better off without her—another example of self-centered thinking. So why didn't I initiate a divorce? I didn't simply because I wanted to be able to claim the high road whenever my children would ask about the divorce. I would be able to self-righteously claim that I hadn't divorced Carolyn. She had divorced me. If the kids were unhappy with that, once again it would be Carolyn's fault. That's it. More self-centered, stinkin' thinkin'.

All of this is background to the day I decided to stay committed to my marriage. I had been sober about nine or ten months at the time. I was once again complaining to my sponsor that my wife didn't appreciate all I was doing for her by getting sober, working the program, and striving for a "personality change sufficient to bring about recovery from alcoholism."[4] He reminded me, once again, that I wasn't doing this for her and that if I were he didn't foresee much success for continued sobriety. That's when he hit me with the comment that the only thing I could do for her and the kids was to commit to a lifetime of making amends by relating to them out of a changed personality. The recovery was for me. The new relationship of respect and care was for them. I objected by asking what good was my commitment to them if, in fact, she might still divorce me. His response was that commitment was up to me. I could commit to a lifetime of amends to them whether I was married or not. I could commit to stay married and give Carolyn the dignity of making her own choice. That was the day I committed to stay married. Divorce was off the table as far as I was concerned.

I had to admit that sometimes I did a pretty poor job of living into and out of the changed personality for which I longed. It was sometimes probably hard for Carolyn to see much change in the way things were from the way they had been. So I bought her a copy of *The Big Book*. She had heard it mentioned often, but I don't think she had ever read it—at least not all of it. In the front of the book I wrote the following inscription:

Dear Carolyn

This book tells my story. For me, it gives me hope for the first time in my life that there is a way for me to live a life of peace and contentment. That hope is something I really never had before. This book describes what I'm trying to become and how I'm trying to do it with God's help. I know that progress will be slow, that I'll never get it quite right, but I trust that things will get better one day at a time if I just don't drink, do the best I can, and trust God.

I want you to have this book because I realize that sometimes my progress, or my direction, or even my intent may not be apparent from my activities because I cannot work this program perfectly. Therefore, this book may help you understand what I'm trying to do and who I'm trying to become.

Love,
Ed

I had done all I could do to commit to our marriage and our family. Now it was up to Carolyn to decide what she would do.

∞

| 7 |
Prayer

The inscription I had written in Carolyn's copy of The Big Book mentioned God twice—both receiving help from him and trusting him. That may seem strange because as yet I didn't believe in God. I was following a precept I had heard spoken in many A.A. meetings: "Fake it 'til you make it." A.A. had been founded in the late 1930s before the cognitive revolution in psychology came to the fore in the 1950s. Behaviorism was held in high regard as a psychological theory in the first half of the twentieth century. Another bit of behaviorist wisdom I had heard often shared in A.A. meetings was the dictum, "I found I couldn't think my way to right living, but I could live my way to right thinking."

Since resolving the "higher power" issue was something I saw as a necessary part of my recovery, I was wont to use God language as The Twelve Steps did. A.A.'s language introduced spirituality in The Twelve Steps in Step Two as "a Power greater than ourselves." Atheists and agnostics in A.A. were told that it was only necessary to believe that a power greater than one's self existed and that recognition that the group itself was greater than one's self was sufficient for spiritual progress to be made. The language of The Twelve Steps then proceeded to narrow the construct for "a power greater than ourselves," first by use of the phrase "God *as we understood Him*" (emphasis in the original) in Step Three and then three uses of a proper noun, "God," or pronoun, "Him," without the qualifying phrase "*as we understood Him*" in Steps Five, Six, and Seven before making the final reference to "God," again with the qualifying phrase "*as we understand Him*" in Step Eleven. But while my lips were saying "God as I understand him" or "God," my heart was saying "God as I don't understand him" or "Whatever helps me make it through today." Mostly, though, I just stuck with "higher power" or "HP" for short.

I made a commitment to stay married by acknowledging it to both myself and to my sponsor. As was typical of my distrustful, fearful heart, I didn't say anything to Carolyn. To my way of twisted thinking, to make that unqualified commitment known to her would have given her ammunition she might use against me in some future verbal battle.

I was now faced with the possibility that nothing would improve. Not a pleasant idea. The next month or so had me often complaining to my sponsor that life in my marriage was miserable and wondering aloud what to do. One day Wally asked me if I prayed for my wife. After a long pause, I said, "No. I don't believe in God." Wally reminded me that he hadn't asked if I believed in God. He had asked if I prayed for my wife. After another long pause, I said, "Wouldn't it be strange to pray to a God I don't believe in?" He replied, "Who cares if it's strange? I think the only way to improve your marriage is to pray for your wife." Another long pause. Then I said, "I wouldn't have a clue as to how to pray." He said, "Just pray for her unqualified happiness." Silence. Finally, I said, "That's stupid. I'm not going to do it." Then Wally responded as he had so often during our sponsoring relationship: He set his jaw, fixed a pugnacious glare on me as only an ex-golden glove boxer, Brooklyn longshoreman can, and muttered through clenched teeth, "Then you just don't want to get well."

I knew that look. It carried the unspoken threat that I could either follow his advice or get another sponsor. I had heard often enough in meetings that often what one doesn't want to do is just what one needs to do. So I mumbled an "I guess so," which drew a "What?" from him. "I guess I'll try praying for my wife," I added. "Don't try. Just do it," was the response. My sincere hope at that point was that my agreement, however half-heartedly expressed, had gotten me off the hook and that we could leave that topic alone in the future.

I saw Wally the next evening at a meeting. I was a little puzzled afterward when he asked me, "How'd it go?" I wasn't sure what he was asking about, so I asked, "How'd what go?" "You know. Praying for your wife." I hemmed and hawed a bit until he said, "You didn't do it, did you?"

I started to stutter a response, something about, "Well, you know I don't believe in God, so it seemed sort of silly." About the time I got to, "Besides…" he stopped me with that familiar stare, clenched his jaw and said, "You just don't want to get well, do you?" Turning on his heel, he stalked away, leaving me with mouth agape and feeling very confused.

The next day was Wednesday so I didn't have to face Wally. Wednesday was his "date night" with his wife. It was with some trepidation that I arrived at my regular Thursday night step meeting. I purposefully didn't arrive early. No since risking another question from Wally. I thought I'd hurry out the door at the end just before we held hands and recited The Lord's Prayer. I avoided eye contact with Wally throughout the meeting, kept my head down and my mouth shut during the discussion, and, as planned, slipped out of the circle at the end before someone could grab my hand. I had sat close to the door, so it was just a matter of a quick turn, a step or two, and I would be out of there.

I made it through the quick turn and bumped headlong into Wally who was standing in the doorway. He waited for the "Amen" and then asked me, "How'd it go?" We did the "But I don't believe in God" dance once more, I got another, "Then you just don't want to get well," and I left. I knew better than to risk another encounter with Wally the next night, so I muttered some kind of a "To whom it may concern" prayer that night and went to sleep feeling embarrassed. That is, I would have muttered it if I had prayed aloud. But I thought prayer of the silent variety was definitely in order.

The next night I answered Wally's question with a "Fine." He said, "Good for you." And then added, "Tell me what you prayed."

I sputtered indignantly, and blustered something about prayer being personal and confidential between a person and God."

"Fogettah 'bout it," he responded in his best Brooklynese. "Youse don't believe in God, so I gotta make sure youse don't mess it up." Like the Borg in the Star Trek movies, resistance was futile. He knew it. I knew it. But that didn't stop me from a half-hearted attempt to avoid the conversation. Eventually I stammered something just to get him to leave me alone.

"No, no. That won't do," he said. "I told you to pray for your wife's unqualified happiness and you prayed, 'Hello, to whoever or whatever's up there, if there is anyone or anything, that is. Would you shape up this obnoxious woman I'm married to so she will see things my way and we can get along?'"

"That's *not* what I said," I said with more energy than I intended.

"Yeah, but that's what you meant," Wally responded.

That began an uncomfortable two weeks. I would see Wally at a meeting my usual four to five times a week. Each time I saw him he'd ask, "How'd it go?" We'd go through variations on our previous conversations until one night after my report he said with a puzzled look on his face, "This ought to be going better."

"See," I said. "Prayer is nothing but a waste of time."

Undeterred, he said, "Tell me how you pray?"

I was close to blowing up. "I just told you what I prayed," I said.

"I didn't ask you *what* you prayed this time. I asked you *how* you prayed."

After a long silence, I realized, once again, that resistance would be futile, so I started in. "Well, Carolyn usually goes to bed first, so I go into the bedroom quietly, get undressed, slip into bed, lie there with my eyes closed, and silently pray…

"That's it. That's the problem," he interrupted me excitedly. "You can't lie in bed and pray. You've got to kneel beside the bed and fold your hands when you pray."

I blew up. "That's the dumbest thing I ever heard," I said. "You've got me praying to a God I don't believe in for unqualified happiness for a woman who hates me, and *now* you want me to make a fool of myself by kneeling beside the bed? 'Fake it 'til you make it' is one thing, but this takes the cake. I won't do it."

Wally calmly replied, "Then you just don't want to get well."

Wally didn't ask me again either what I prayed or how I prayed. I should have felt relieved. Instead I knew I had skated onto thin ice. One night a few days later, I knelt by the side of my bed and gave prayer another try. I continued night after night and nothing seemed to be happening. One night, Carolyn woke up while I was kneeling beside the bed and asked, "Are you alright?" "Yeah, just praying," I muttered. I was beyond embarrassed to be caught praying. I was humiliated.

By this time I was going to church regularly but still alone. I guess when Carolyn saw me praying that night she must have figured that maybe I was seriously seeking to find God after all. Slowly things changed. She and the kids started coming to church with me. I thought we were managing to be a little more civil to each other. Then one day, the bomb hit.

Like many arguments, I can't remember what we were talking about or what started it. I was sitting at the kitchen table and Carolyn was standing across the room between the stove and the sink. Suddenly, she erupted. I heard about how even in recovery how self-centered I still was. It was always all about me. *Ed's* getting sober; *Ed's* doing so well; Ed's *still* never home, it's just now that he's at a meeting instead of a bar; It's always about *Ed.* Then the volume increased and she began to say over and over, "When's it going to be *my* turn? When's it going to be *my* turn?" while she pounded her fists on the counter top. I didn't know what to say. Suddenly she stopped abruptly, as suddenly as if she'd been shot. I was afraid. I thought she might have had a heart attack. I was waiting for her to drop to the floor. Instead, after a pause, she just calmly said, "Oh, it *is* my turn. It's just not like I thought it would be."

Carolyn had a fantasy of what life would be like if I just didn't drink. She thought if I just didn't drink, life would be great. Well, I wasn't drinking, hadn't for almost a year, and life definitely wasn't great. Though figuratively rather than literally, her fantasy involved me coming home at five P.M., carrying my lunchbox up the front walk through the white picket fence that surrounded a cute little bungalow, yelling, "Hi, Honey—I'm home," greeting her with a kiss, and asking, "How was your day?"

One of the sayings I'd heard at meetings was that resentments are formed on unmet expectations. The only way to let go of resentment was to let go of the expectation. I don't know if she let go of her expectations of what life would be like with me in that moment, but something changed. I could sense that while she might still have preferences for how I should act and respond, she realized that I was me and that she had to come to grips with who I was rather than hope that someday I would suddenly become the person she wanted me to be. In a way it was like an Al-Anon first step. Whereas in Alcoholics Anonymous the first step is admitting that one was powerless over alcohol and that one's life had become unmanageable, in Al-Anon the first step is often stated as admitting that one was powerless over the alcoholic in one's life and that one's life is unmanageable.

The issue is control. The alcoholic can't control his or her drinking and the spouse can't control the alcoholic. "Control" is one of the three Cs that those in Al-Anon have to struggle against. They must realize they didn't cause the addiction, they can't cure it, and they can't control the alcoholic/addict in their life. These admissions form the core of what is meant by "surrender." The fight is over. While there's still hard work to be done, we give up on the task of trying to run the world according to our likings.

I don't know if that was the moment Carolyn committed to our marriage as I had a few months before, but a few nights later, another strange thing happened. I was kneeling beside my bed, praying for my wife's unqualified happiness when I suddenly became very aware that I really did want Carolyn to be happy. She had let go of expecting that I make her happy and now I simply wanted her to be happy.

I came to the conclusion that this prayer is strange stuff. I still didn't believe in God. I didn't know if the God I didn't believe in was changing Carolyn just as someone or something was changing me. What I did know is that the process of praying had changed me.

Out of the blue, I remembered something that had happened about seven years before. Our son had contracted bacterial spinal meningitis just before his fifth birthday. It was touch and go. He spent nineteen days in isolation before we were able to see him. This was before bio-suits and when gowning and gloving were considered too risky around meningitis except for essential medical personnel. I bought two cases of scotch whiskey and stayed drunk the whole time while we waited first for word that he would make it, and then, for the disease to run its course.

The night we took him into the hospital, the doctors did a spinal tap and diagnosed meningitis. As they wheeled him on a gurney to his isolation room, my wife grabbed me by the arm and pushed me up against the wall in the hospital corridor. She said, "You pray for him." I started to explain that I didn't believe in God and that prayer was a waste of time, but she'd have none of it. "You were raised in the church. You know how to pray. Now you pray!" I knew better than to argue at that point. So I prayed for my son. I have no idea the details of what I prayed, but I vaguely remember the typical, "If you'll save my son, I'll serve you." I sometimes think God takes our prayers seriously even when we don't. This prayer is strange stuff.

∞

| 8 |
The Great Warm Fuzzy

Against my will, I had learned how to pray. I now half-believed in the effectiveness of this strange practice. After all, something had changed in Carolyn, me, and our marriage once consistent prayer for her unqualified happiness had become my daily routine. Now where should I go from here? I still didn't believe in God. If pressed about how I thought prayer could work if there was no God, I would have simply shrugged my shoulders and shook my head.

The church we were attending was a fairly good-sized one of about fifteen hundred people. It was solidly Evangelical even though it was part of an old, established denomination. The denomination had drifted away from vibrant faith toward nominalism. But in our congregation, old-fashioned piety exemplified by daily devotions, prayer groups, and Adult Sunday School classes were part of our culture. We were part of an Adult Sunday School class, as much, in my opinion, to form friendships within the church community as to learn anything. My critical nature always had a hundred questions when a Bible lesson was presented, but while the person presenting the lesson always encouraged questions, hard questions and debate were considered rude. So I just basically listened and bit my tongue.

I had learned the power of group experiences in A.A., so I availed myself of a men's small group that met for mutual encouragement and prayer at 6:30 on Wednesday mornings. Having never been a "morning person," I thought God, if there were one, would really be impressed with my dedication and discipline even though devotion wasn't really part of my life because I didn't believe in him.

All I knew about prayer was what my sponsor Wally had forced me into and the experiences that had occurred as I followed his directions. I wasn't about to confess my inadequacies on the subject of prayer in this group by asking for advice. I was afraid that a question like, "Is it OK to pray if you don't believe in God?" would provoke an Evangelical feeding frenzy to get me saved. Yes, I wanted to explore spiritual issues, but on my own terms and at my own pace. My hope was that I could learn something from the group just by observation.

What I learned was that spending an hour in prayer was boring and that it seemed that unless you ended your prayer with "in Jesus' name" you didn't have a prayer that your prayer would be answered. One of the guys in the group took me aside and said as much. I started ending my prayers with "in Jesus' name," but I felt like a hypocrite. So I stopped concluding my prayers with the supposedly essential phrase. He mentioned it to me once or twice more and then gave up on me. I noticed, however, that when I would end my prayer without the magic words he would whisper them loud enough for me—and I assume the others—to hear. I began to take a perverse pride in my obstinate refusal to conform.

I thought about quitting the group, but I didn't know how to leave it without provoking a bunch of unwanted inquiries about what was missing in my spiritual life, why that group wasn't meeting my needs, and evoking suggestions about what other groups I might try. Negotiating the tricky waters of church protocol is hard work for the uninitiated.

That left daily devotions, or "quiet time," to round out my expected compliance with the minimum requirements of acceptable church life. Adult Sunday School and the men's small group prayer meeting were my attempts to conform to church practices with church materials. The idea of daily devotions, by myself, using religious materials I didn't understand, left me nonplussed, however. So I decided to construct my own version of daily devotions. I'd set aside the time and place but I'd use some A.A. related material.

In church, I had heard the mysterious suggestion to go to one's "prayer closet" for prayer. In a sermon, Fred had explained that it wasn't really a literal closet, but rather a specific time and place to pray where one could have relative peace and quiet. I knew just the spot. Our living room faced east and had big windows with wide-slat plantation shutters. Just beneath the windows was a comfy white canvas sectional. I could nestle into the corner of the sectional and do my devotions while the morning sunlight streamed through the shutters.

The material I decided to use was *Twenty-Four Hours a Day*.[1] I had heard a lot of A.A. folks mention it at various meetings. While not official A.A. literature, it was widely used by A.A. members at the meetings I attended. It was a small book: about 5 ¾ by 3 ½ inches. It had one page for each day of the year. Each page began with an "A.A. Thought for the Day," followed by a "Meditation for the

Day" and a "Prayer for the Day." The "A.A. Thought for the Day" had a statement regarding alcoholism or recovery and usually concluded with a question or series of questions prompted by the topic. The "Meditation for the Day" expanded on the topic in a reflective way and prompted contemplation on the topic more by being thought provoking rather than by asking direct questions. The "Thought" and the "Meditation" were of approximate equal length and together took up 75 to 80 percent of the page. The "Prayer" was by far the shortest part, rarely exceeding two sentences.

I liked the shortness of the prayers. It fit my experience of how effective prayer works. The prayer topic Wally had given me was short, sweet, and to the point: "Pray for your wife's unqualified happiness." Nothing fancy. Easy to stay focused. I was to pray it until I could pray it with conviction that it truly expressed the desire of my heart.

I developed a four-day a week routine. Wednesday I was at the men's small group prayer meeting organized by the church. There I experienced corporate prayer. Saturday I took the day off. Sunday was already spiritual enough with church. Monday, Tuesday, Thursday, and Friday I'd open the shutters, park my butt on the couch, open the book to the page for the day, and start in. The questions in the "thought" portion could often be answered with "yes" or "no." That didn't require too long. The "meditation" portion sometimes provoked me to some reflection and sometimes didn't. Then I'd repeat the "prayer" to myself a few times.

It was hard to stretch this routine much beyond two or three minutes. Somehow I didn't think that was worthy of qualifying as a daily devotional. So I began to improvise. I started asking myself questions that the book didn't ask.

For example, the first page, to be read on January 1, asks:

> When I came into A.A., was I a desperate person? Did
> I have a soul-sickness? Was I so sick of myself and my
> way of living that I couldn't stand looking at myself in a
> mirror? Was I ready for A.A.? Was I ready to try anything
> that would help me to get sober and to get over my soul-
> sickness? *Should I ever forget the condition I was in?*[2]

Six questions; six answers: yes, maybe (I wasn't sure
anyone had a soul), hmm, yes, yes (if I ignored the "soul
sickness" part), and I'm not sure (is this a trick question?).

After proceeding for several weeks and deciding I had
to beef up my devotions, I tried elaborating on the answers
and letting the questions provoke additional questions. I
might begin to read the "A.A. Thought for the Day" like
this: "When I came into A.A., was I a desperate person?"

Yes. How do I know that? I was ready to kill myself. Really? Well as close as I ever want to come to it.

"Was I so sick of myself and my way of living that I
couldn't stand looking at myself in a mirror?"

Hmm. Why am I hesitating on this? Maybe it's the mirror part. That's not been literally true for me. So, what has
been true that's giving me pause? Loathing comes to mind.
I live with self-loathing. I like to drink but I don't like not
being able to stop when a normal person would have had
enough. Weak-willed _____ (please supply a
litany of offensive profanities here). Yup, self-loathing. Not
self-pity. That's different. What's lurking behind the loathing? Anger. Actually, more like rage. I would get so pissed-
off at myself I couldn't stand it. Angry at myself. Didn't
I hear somewhere that depression is anger turned inward?
Was I or am I depressed? I've always felt down. So let's see,
self-medicate for depression by consuming alcohol, a sed-
ative drug. Not the sharpest knife in the drawer. Stupid.

Gee, that comment will start another round of self-loathing. And on, and on.

"Should I ever forget the condition I was in?"

If I don't forget what my life was like, will the rest of my life be wallowing in the shame and regret of the past? Can there be happiness if I'm constantly reminded of my hopelessness? Or was George Santayana right: "Those who cannot remember the past are condemned to repeat it."[3]

Then on to the Meditation for the Day: "In the new year, I will live one day at a time…"

Well, that is the A.A. mantra: "One day at a time." I guess it should remind me that change may be slow, but will surely come if I just stay at it. "Rome wasn't built in a day" and all that. Doesn't The Big Book say to look for "spiritual progress rather than spiritual perfection?"[4] No more getting down on myself. Is "One day at a time" the antidote for self-loathing? I've got to remember that getting sober is like eating an elephant. You eat an elephant one bite at a time; you get sober one day at a time.

"…I will make each day one of preparation for better things ahead…"

OK, what can I work on today beyond my family and job "have to"s that will prepare me to live better? Boy, there's a list of a thousand things! But that's the problem. I always tackle too much, get overwhelmed, start to fail, and throw the whole thing out. Maybe the secret is just picking one thing and sticking to it. Eureka! What's the one thing that would make the biggest improvement in me and my life? Maybe I should talk with my sponsor about that. Wally got me praying, but this sounds more like a conversation for Clyde. He's the "spiritual type." Ah, there's the problem. I just said to myself, "Maybe I should talk with Clyde." Why "maybe?" Isn't procrastination one of my big problems? OK, definitely. I'll see Clyde at the meeting tonight and start the conversation.

The meditation continued:

> I will not dwell on the past or the future, only on the present. I will bury every fear of the future, all thoughts of unkindness and bitterness, all my dislikes, my resentments, my sense of failure, my disappointments in others and in myself, my gloom and my despondency.

Hoo-boy! That's sure got me pegged. "Sense of failure... disappointments... gloom... despondency..." Has someone been reading my mail? That's just what I was thinking about. Am I really afraid of the future? Afraid of failing? What's up with that?

The "Prayer for the Day" for January 1 is a simple two sentences: "I pray that God will guide me one day at a time in the new year. I pray that for each day, God will supply the wisdom and the strength that I need."

Nice. Simple. I could say the words, but were they just words or were they truly a prayer? When I was following Wally's instructions night after night, I tried to go beyond rote repetition. But how do you make yourself believe something? I could sweat and strain all I wanted, change the silent inflection of my inner voice, try to be sincere, but I couldn't make myself mean it. It took me over a month of praying for Carolyn's unqualified happiness before one night I felt the difference. What I couldn't make myself believe, I finally came to believe honestly and sincerely. Did I just talk myself into it? Or had repetition changed my heart? Was there really a God and if so, was he involved in the change? I knew something had changed through that prayer exercise. I just didn't know how the change had occurred. What I did know was the process I had gone through faithfully until one day the change happened.

So I had a roadmap for prayer in my daily devotions. I would simply repeat the prayer for the day over and over, adding any other thoughts that were prompted by the prayer. I would try to make myself mean what I was saying, just like I had when I was praying for Carolyn's unqualified happiness. Usually it was just five minutes or so of repetition. But with the additional time and attention in the "Thought for the Day" and "Meditation" sections, I was now up to fifteen or twenty minutes each morning. I also began to pray a paraphrase of the Prayer for the Day silently throughout the day. I felt more like I was making a respectable attempt at this daily devotion thing.

Sometimes I would find that I had actually spent twenty to thirty minutes in my spiritual exercises. On those days it seemed like it wasn't the result of a conscious attempt to extend my time. It's just that some days, somewhere in the process, I would begin to feel a sense of peace envelop me. When that happened, I didn't have to try to stay at it longer. I just did. I find it hard to describe the feeling that would creep over me at those times. The closest I can come was that it was a warm and fuzzy feeling—sort of a combination of warm flannel pajamas just out of the clothes dryer and the drifting feeling experienced just before sleep. I often enter a state when I go to bed where I don't know if I'm asleep or awake. I'm thinking thoughts, but I'm not sure I'm in conscious control of the thoughts. It feels almost like I'm dreaming or as if I'm listening to someone else think thoughts for me. At those times I would have the same sense of wellbeing that would now occasionally steal into my daily devotions.

I began to enjoy the times that this feeling would happen. In fact, I began to long for it to occur. I found myself inviting it—the feeling, whatever it was—to share my time as I started my daily devotions. It seemed that my invitation resulted in it happening more often. The feeling was almost palpable. I began to think of it as a presence that I didn't have a name for. So I invented one. I called it The Great Warm Fuzzy. One day it dawned on me that maybe this was an encounter with a "Higher Power" that was often talked about in A.A. Those in A.A. who were trying to be cute or cool sometimes referred to this Higher Power as HP. So, in my private thoughts, I sometimes referred to this great warm fuzzy feeling as GWF. I didn't talk to anyone about this. I thought it sounded crazy enough that it might draw strange glances and condescending looks. But the mornings when I felt it began to increase to the point that it happened almost every time I took my place in my "prayer closet."

Sometime in the process I began to add one other thing. Just before quitting my devotions for the day, I began a little exercise to "come up slowly" from the embrace of Great Warm Fuzzy. I'd begin to go over my upcoming day in my mind and think about what I had on my agenda. Items that I felt unsure of or unsettled about, I would "hand over" to The Great Warm Fuzzy. I could feel the unsettledness and discomfort leave me as I did so. I still had to take them on that day, but I felt like I had "turned them over" to GWF and I could quit worrying about them. Than I could enter my day with serenity and gratitude that GWF would take care of the tough ones. If it didn't seem like he did, it would be because nothing could be done. All I had to do was take care of what I could handle and just show up for the rest. Is this what is meant by "Let go and let God?"

This was back in the late 1970s. One of the hot topics in "relaxation therapy" was visualization. In the rehab program, we had gone through guided visualizations several times a week to help us learn to keep our emotions under control. There was much talk about "finding your happy place" or "your safe place" and being able to go there mentally when times got tough. This was also the era when sports celebrities were talking about visualization. Basketball players talked about visualizing the ball going swish through the net as they released the shot. Golfers talked about visualizing the break of the ball just as they stroked the putt. Somehow I began a practice of visualization as I went through my day's agenda, selecting what I could handle and what I'd turn over to the Great Warm Fuzzy. The things I could handle I'd visualize putting in my pocket. The ones that had me uncertain and unsettled I'd set to one side. When I was done sorting the list, I'd visualize myself gathering up the problems I had to face that day that I had set to one side, molding them into a ball, and rolling that ball away from me—toward The Great Warm Fuzzy, I guess. Then with a sigh of contentment and confidence, I'd conclude my daily devotions, get up from the couch, and head into my day.

This had been going on for several weeks with me feeling better and better about my morning devotions. I felt like I was engaged in A.A.'s eleventh step in which I "sought to establish conscious contact with God, *as [I] understood Him…*" One day, something happened that stunned me. I had thought my A.A. Thought for the Day, meditated on my Meditation for the Day, prayed my Prayer for the Day, and slipped into the peaceful embrace of Great Warm Fuzzy. I concluded my sorting through my agenda for the day; pocketing the things I could handle; setting aside what I couldn't handle; molding my fears, uncertainties, and doubts into a ball; and rolled it away toward Great Warm Fuzzy in anticipation of the feeling of serenity with which I would then enter my day. Without warning, I suddenly sensed my ball of fear, uncertainty, and doubt being pushed back toward me by Great Warm Fuzzy. I was startled to "hear" a voice say to me, "I want all of you or I'll take none of you."

I write "hear" because I don't know how else to describe it. It wasn't as if I had heard an audible voice. It was more like I hadn't been paying attention but something like a voice broke though and got my attention. It was an experience that seemed like remembering the words I would have heard had I been paying attention. It's like a memory lay on the surface of my mind of something I had heard, but I didn't recall actually hearing it. C. S. Lewis does as good a job as any I've encountered in capturing the sense of certainty shrouded in ambiguity of this mystical sort of hearing.

> It was as though the voice which had called to me from the world's end were now speaking at my side. It was with me in the room, or in my own body, or behind me. If it had once eluded me by its distance, it now eluded me by proximity— something too near to see, too plain to be understood, on this side of knowledge. It seemed to have been always with me; if I could ever have turned my head quick enough I should have seized it. Now for the first time I felt that it was out of reach not because of something I could not do but because of something I could not stop doing. If I could only leave off, let go, unmake myself, it would be there.[5]

I was stunned. This wasn't what I had signed up for. The last month or more had brought me to a place of my daily devotions being life-giving to me. I would feed my soul (if I had one), contemplate spiritual questions, pray, receive peace and serenity, get rid of the nagging fears prompted by upcoming situations in my day, and get on with life. And now this. I felt like Great Warm Fuzzy had suckered me into something. He had set me up. Lured me into reliance upon him only so he could spring the trap and demand more of me than I was willing to give. I began to have the sneaky suspicion that I had been had by this Higher Power that some chose to call God.

I continued my daily devotional practices. I didn't know what else to do. But deep down I knew my bluff of playing at life on my terms had been called. I began to realize that the poker game called Texas Hold 'Em was a pretty good metaphor for life with God, if that's who Great Warm Fuzzy really was.

If you don't know the game, it's a version of seven-card stud with each player holding two hole cards and the dealer turning up a series of five cards played in common by all the players. As the cards are turned over, checks, bets, raises, and calls go around the table, growing the pot. Like most poker games, a great deal of the money is made not by holding winning hands, but rather by betting in ways that make others *think* you are holding a winning hand. Calculating the probability of holding a winning hand may be the science of poker, but bluffing is the art of the game. The strongest bet a player can offer either in confidence he or she has the winning hand or to risk the biggest bluff is to go "all in." The player pushes every chip in front of him or her into the pot and says, "I'm all in." These bets are usually of considerable size. They are always of considerable importance. The other players think long and hard before calling such a bet. If you win the "all in," you're usually sitting pretty. You may have busted another player out of the game if they thought you were bluffing but you weren't. But if you lose an "all in" bet, you're out of the game. Busted.

Here's the irony of the "all in" bet. You'd think that if you win it, you'd be home free. But winning an "all in" bet just means that sometime later in the game you'll have to go "all in" again—and again, and again—until, finally, winner takes all. I had just found out that God, if that's who it was, is one hell of a poker player. I thought I had gone all in by starting the practice of daily devotions that led me to trusting the feeling of some unseen entity more than I ever thought I could. That risk for me was going "all in" at the time. Then, just when I thought I had things under control, just when I was beginning to like this Great Warm Fuzzy fellow, he pulled the rug out from under me. He upped the ante. He changed the rules. Of course they were my rules, and he had never agreed to play by them, but he had been acquiescing and I took that as agreement. I was blindsided when he suddenly decided to stop playing by my rules. Lewis says it bluntly. "God is, if I may say it, very unscrupulous."[6] It's almost as if we ought to rewrite the old hymn that says "What a mighty God we serve!"[7] and change the words to "What a sneaky God we serve!" Maybe that's why God chose Jacob instead of Esau. He admired his cunning. (Ge 25.19-34; 27.1-33; 28.10-22)

Now I had a decision to make. I could quit playing, abandon my sunny little spot on the couch four mornings of the week, and take my fears, uncertainties, and doubts back onto my shoulders, or I could go all in again and give God—that's who I was beginning to suspect the Great Warm Fuzzy was—the parts of my life in which I didn't think I needed him. I wondered what to do for several days. Then one day during the next week, I didn't sort through my agenda. I went through it, acknowledged every element of it, both what I thought I could handle and what I was afraid I couldn't, and handed it all to Great Warm Fuzzy, saying, "Here it is. All of it. All of me. Take it. I'm all in." That became my daily practice.

∞

| 9 |
Because That's Just
The Way It Is

Things in life are often different than one would wish them to be. One of the changes that has occurred in me as life keeps adding years onto my age is that I seem to be developing a different response to this reality. When younger, in a much more idealistic, altruistic frame of mind, I would struggle against the way things were with a vengeance, as if I could change life to conform to my image of what should be by dint of the intensity of my opposition.

It was this "stand against the wind" attitude that caused me to lurch to a stop, when, as a kid in high school, I was reading Earl Thompson's *A Garden of Sand*.[1] The protagonist is Jacky, a child of the depression growing up in a hugely dysfunctional family. He's a fighter against long odds in the manner that I'm describing as "struggling against the way things are." Bill Wild, an unlikely father figure to Jacky, uses a phrase that, when I first read it, I thought surely must be a misprint: "It's a hard life if you don't weaken." By the end of the book, however, the statement had reappeared four or five times. It wasn't a misprint.

I was much more of the mindset at that time that it was a hard life if you *did* weaken. To weaken meant that life would ride over you roughshod. Fate, or whatever you'd like to call it, would take you, break you, and make you into something less than you imagined yourself to be. I aspired to be much more like the heroic figure evoked by Hamlet's phrase, "take arms against a sea of troubles, and by opposing, end them."[2] It was only later that I observed that it was the mighty, stalwart oaks from which gusts of wind snapped limbs or even uprooted them entirely. It was the grass that bent to the wind that survived.

Youth is filled with much "wisdom" that age later proves to be less than wise. As I grow older, I'm affected by encroaching reality much as the desert fox was in a parable by Kahlil Gibran in *The Madman*.

> A fox looked at his shadow at sunrise and said, "I will have a camel for lunch today." And all morning he went about looking for camels. But at noon he saw his shadow again and said, "A mouse will do."[3]

I was getting acquainted with God in the persona of The Great Warm Fuzzy. When he rolled my ball of problems I felt I couldn't handle back to me one morning, I encountered something I did not like. He was changing my rules. He was going to dictate how the game between us would be played. I didn't like it. It reminded me of something my spiritual sponsor, Clyde, had once said. I was going on about something that wasn't to my liking. He said, "You're angry, I see." "No," I replied. "I'm just frustrated." He responded, "There is no such thing as frustration. What we call frustration is simply our being angry that we're not God and, therefore, can't have everything our way." I filed that away with another of his *bon mots*: "A problem is just something not going the way you want it to." I wasn't sure I liked either of his sage observations.

God not shaping reality to conform to my expectations of what should be opened the floodgates to things that had driven me away from him when I was in my early teens. I was upset by "the problem of evil." Sometimes called "theodicy," the problem of evil states that belief in a sovereign God who possessed the commonly acknowledged attributes of complete goodness and complete power (omnipotence) is illogical if one recognizes that evil exists. Sovereign means that God can do anything he wants. Therefore, either God is not completely good because he has the power to eradicate evil, but does not act to do so. Or God is not all-powerful because he wills to eradicate evil but is unable to do so. Stuck with a God who was compromised either in his goodness or his power, I simply chucked the whole idea of God.

Another idea that gave me pause in my youth was the exclusivity of Jesus. He was *the* way, *the* truth, and *the* life. No one could come to God except through him. (Jn 14.6) Later, I would hear this described as "the scandal of particularity." If one gives credence to a hypothetical total number of *homo sapiens* who have ever lived and divides that number into the 144,000 mentioned in Revelation (Re 14.3), the portion of humanity that will make it into heaven is a dismal 1.44×10^{-6}. Even though the number 144,000 is probably either hypothetical or symbolic, I still infer that the majority of people who have ever lived have never heard about Jesus and therefore will not be among those who will be "redeemed from the earth." (Re 14.3) Are they irretrievably lost because they were born in the wrong time or wrong place?

Paul seems to acknowledge the problem when he asks, "how can they believe in the one of whom they have not heard?" (Ro 10.14) So, what of all those who have never heard of Christ? Were they doomed by an accident of birth?

My early roots in the Lutheran Church revealed a God who rather arbitrarily would "have mercy on whom I have mercy, and...have compassion on whom I have compassion." (Ex 33.19) This didn't seem fair. Paul had also written that when people "do by nature things required" by God they are "a law unto themselves." (Ro 2.14) Is that option still open? If, back in the day, someone who hadn't heard about Jesus could be all right with God by following his or her conscience, what about someone who had heard about Jesus, but just couldn't buy the so-called Gospel for whatever reason? How could God say he "does not show favoritism" (Ac 10.34) if one group has found a non-Jesus way in and another is kept out?

These were the questions that were reasserting themselves into my thoughts about a God that I still didn't believe in, but who was being more winsome under the guise of Great Warm Fuzzy. I certainly hadn't wanted to engage these questions again. But my search for a Higher Power had led me back to the God question. My search for answers to the God question had led me back to church. And church was full of Jesus talk. I felt the God I had abandoned twenty years before had ambushed me.

I can remember one morning in this period of searching when I engaged Great Warm Fuzzy in the Jesus question. I don't remember how it had come to the forefront of my thoughts that morning. I had been going through my morning meditation routine. I was cloaked in the comfortable embrace of Great Warm Fuzzy. Somehow I had begun thinking about where Jesus was going to fit into all this if, in fact, he was going to fit in at all. I can clearly remember the vehemence with which I was engaging with God. Over and over in my mind I was repeating, "But why does it have to be Jesus? But why does it have to be Jesus?" It was a strange moment. There I was, arguing with a God I wasn't sure existed. Yet strangely, like Job, I felt at liberty to question the

Almighty. God's response to Job was a thunderous answer out of a storm:

> Who is this that darkens my counsel
> with words without knowledge?
> Brace yourself like a man;
> I will question you,
> and you shall answer me. (Jb 38.2-3)

The answer that came to me began with a physical sensation. The embracing warmth of Great Warm Fuzzy slowly changed to an iron grip like cold, hard steel and a chill that penetrated to my bones. I still don't know if I heard an audible voice in the next few moments, but I had the clear impression that God, or whoever it was, had said, "Because that's just the way it is." The impression of any physical sensation whether warmly embracing me or coldly griping me slowly faded away and I was alone. I mean, really alone.

As I've told other Christians this part of my story, many of them don't like it. It doesn't fit with the image of the God they know. At some point, we Jesus followers will have to come to grips with the worst implications of the phrase "the fear of the Lord." We have come to regard God Almighty as a cosmic magician who will work wonders to alleviate our discomfort. After he's done so, we wish he would just politely go away until we need him again. Or he's become our "Buddy Jesus," as described by a priest played by George Carlin in the movie *Dogma*. God does work wonders on our behalf, even the normal wonders we describe as common grace by which "He causes the sun to rise on the evil and the good, and sends rain on the righteous and the unrighteous." (Mt 5.45) As the hymn says, we do have a friend in Jesus. But we must remember that "awful" and "awesome" are related etymologically. Awe may be inspired by that which is terrible as well as that which is beautiful. It is only when we can recognize the fearsomeness of our

God that his unqualified love, forgiveness, acceptance, redemption, and reconciliation of us become awe inspiring in ways that are awesome. It's a principle akin to the adage that "Our 'yes' is meaningless until we can also say 'no.'" Truly, God is merciful, but as Sheldon Vanauken observed in the title of his book, sometimes it's *A Severe Mercy*. But "the hardness of God is kinder than the softness of men."[4]

My life to that point had been lived in a "stand against the wind" rebellion that refused to believe that I couldn't change reality to meet my beliefs of what should be. Yet, in that moment, two thoughts were indelibly etched into my understanding. First, I could try as hard as I might but I was not going to change God's view of things. "[His] ways were not [my] ways" and because "[his] thoughts were not [my] thoughts" (Is 55.8), I might never understand why things are the way they are. The second was that if I chose not to surrender to his reality, I would live my life alone.

This thought was strange in that my experience told me that I didn't have to believe in God or accept his ways to have people around me. I had lived that way for the past twenty years. But my experience also showed me the hollowness of my protest. I could have people around me and yet be alone in a crowd. I had spent most of my life in that condition. There is a big difference between seclusion and being isolated. Seclusion brings rest, restoration, and silent strength. Isolation brings a sense of abandonment, unwanted vulnerability, and night terrors.

Like so many times in the spiritual journey I was on, I hadn't planned a watershed moment for that morning. It seemed like that in admitting that I couldn't control my drinking I had truly come to understand that there was precious little—if anything—I could control. Was this what it meant to take the second part of the first step? The first step begins with we "admitted we were powerless over alcohol…" I had pretty deeply assimilated that truth and incorporated it into a new view of reality: I couldn't drink any more. Alcohol would take over in a way characterized by a Japanese proverb that had been converted to poetry by Edward Rowland Sill:

> At the punch bowl's brink,
> Let the thirsty think,
> What they say in Japan:
> First the man takes a drink,
> Then the drink takes a drink,
> Then the drink takes the man.[5]

It's the conclusion to the first step that at first seems hard to acknowledge: "that our lives had become unmanageable." I don't think I am alone in not wanting to see myself as incompetent to manage my own affairs. After all, didn't most of us grow up yelling "You're not the boss of me" to siblings and playmates? Isn't there a shred of dignity to which I can cling? Something that I can handle? Then it hit me. My encounter with Great Warm Fuzzy in which he rolled my ball of problems back to me with the declaration, "I'll take all of you or I'll take none of you" had set me up for this encounter. The question was, who was going to be in control? I saw why I had been having such a problem with this second part of "the surrender step." My combative and rebellious nature seemed to always respond to propositions as if they were challenges. It was always fight or flight, never "Hmm, that might be right." If it wasn't my idea, I feared I would lose control of the situation. I would simply be a pawn in another's game. I didn't like that way of seeing myself in relation to anyone else, not even God.

It was many years later that I was able to better understand the foundational problem. One cannot read much of Jesus in the Gospels without encountering the phrase "the kingdom of God." The word "kingdom" often elicits unhelpful associations with the idea of realm or place. The kingdom of God is not that kind of kingdom. As Jesus said to Pilate, "My kingdom is not of this world." (Jn 18.36) I've found it more helpful to use the phrase "the kingship of God." By "kingship" I mean the status that gives someone a legitimate right to rule. This puts the issue squarely on the table. Either God both rules and reigns in my life or he doesn't. Any attempt to negotiate a better deal with God gives the impression that I believe God's sovereignty is somehow limited. If I can just find a crack into which to drive the thin edge of the wedge, I can gain an advantage. We would become like two hustlers jockeying for position.

What this means, of course, is that at some level I would consider myself an equal with God, able to negotiate as a peer. It is a manifestation of a sin defined by the first commandment. God said, "I am the LORD your God… You shall have no other gods besides me." (Ex 20.2-3. Alternative translation) Refusal to surrender to God's rule and reign without reservation means that I've rejected the idea of the kingship of God and decided that I can run my own life. That path leads nowhere good. As George MacDonald has written, "The one principle of hell is—'I am my own.'"[6] I was beginning the transition to surrender. Strangely, I found myself in unfamiliar territory, but not frightened by the prospect of surrender. I was moving from "that can't be" to "it is what it is." My response to life was moving from "I'll show you" to "deal with it."

I may not like that Great Warm Fuzzy had said that Jesus was "just the way it is," but my options were clearly either to accept and submit to that reality or to reject it and move on into life alone. Negotiation for a different deal was not an option. I wasn't ready to make a decision, but I knew what the choices were.

∞

Surprise!

My first A.A. birthday came and went. One year of so-briety. Or as my sponsors often reminded me, one year without a drink. Sobriety comes later, as a result of working the program, they would say. Otherwise, a person is just on a dry drunk. Not drinking, but full of the self-centeredness, self-pity, resentments, expectations, and blaming that often characterize alcoholics and other addicts. Maybe resentments and expectations are a redundancy. Someone once said that expectations are resentments waiting to happen. How long would it take to attain sobriety?

I was not sure I wanted to ask my sponsors, especially Wally, who was known to string his "babies" along a bit. In rehab, they had stressed the importance of attaining the milestone of collecting a thirty-day "chip"—a token pre-sented at an A.A. meeting signifying thirty days of absti-nence, which was often generously referred to as sobriety. The prescription for making that happen was often expressed as going to thirty meetings in thirty days and not drinking between meetings. When I got my thirty-day chip, Wally, who was not yet my sponsor, leaned over to me and said,

"Congratulations. The real winners go to sixty meetings in sixty days and they don't drink between meetings." Thirty days later, as I collected my sixty-day chip, Wally leaned over to me and said, "Congratulations. The real winners go to ninety meetings in ninety days and they don't drink between meetings." It was then I decided to ask him to be my sponsor. He pissed me off just enough to generate an "I'll show you" attitude in me that had always helped me succeed in the past. I knew that we get sober for ourselves rather than for anyone else, but finding motivation wherever one could was not a bad strategy.

Wally became my sponsor, but when I took my one-year chip, I was not about to ask him how long before I could consider myself sober instead of just dry. Talk in rehab had mentioned a two-year period of continuous abstinence as a typical turn-around time period to clear away the wreckage of the past and to find one's way into a new way of life, one that could be described as sober while in pursuit of the ever-desired, but elusive, serenity.

I was still unsure of the God question, but I was to the point of having almost undeniable suspicions. I had come to realize that honesty was the essential starting point for the program of recovery suggested in the twelve steps. Without honesty, responsibilities could be shirked, resentments linger, relationships remain estranged, shortcomings remain unacknowledged, character defects denied or ignored, amends left unmade, and apologies unextended. Without honesty— a recognition and acceptance of reality—I could remain in a world of my own devising where I was wronged but did no wrong, misunderstood but never understanding, and taking but never giving without expectation of recompense, living exactly in the opposite spirit of the prayer of St. Francis. To be honest, I had to realize that I wasn't the center of the universe. It all didn't center on and revolve around me.

It's said that nature abhors a vacuum. So does the soul. Four hundred years ago, Pascal spoke of a human craving described as an infinite abyss that only an infinite and immutable entity can fulfill.

> What else does this craving, and this helplessness, proclaim but that there was once in [humans] a true happiness, of which all that now remains is the empty [im]print and trace? This [we try] in vain to fill with everything around [us] … though none can help, since this infinite abyss can be filled only with an infinite and immutable object; in other words by God himself.[1]

Pascal may well have found his inspiration for the idea in St. Augustine's Confessions where the fourth century African saint said to God, "You have made us for yourself, and our hearts are restless 'til they find their rest in you."[2]

Our modern paraphrase of this "infinite abyss" that only God can fill is the "God-shaped hole" or "God-shaped vacuum" that exists in the human soul. But did I have a soul? To answer "Yes" would open the door to a separate reality that could be described as "spiritual." Once open to the possibility of a realm of spirit, the possibility of an overarching Spirit had to be acknowledged. The possibility of God loomed on the horizon.

It was only later that I encountered the idea that there really wasn't a separate spiritual dimension through an Alfred Edersheim quote: "To the secular [person] there is nothing spiritual; but to the spiritual [person] there is nothing secular."[3] This conveyed the integration of the spiritual with all of life. It parallels an anecdote told in A.A. about Dr. Bob, one of the co-founders of Alcoholics Anonymous. Supposedly, a newcomer had mentioned to Dr. Bob that he liked the program, but really didn't get the spiritual part. Dr. Bob reportedly replied, "There is no spiritual part. It's a spiritual program." If God is to fill the God-shaped hole in one's soul, he uses the opportunity to insert himself into every aspect of a person's life.

I was no longer satisfied with describing the emotions I was getting in touch with as merely the effect of chemical interactions triggered by neurological electrical impulses. Descartes said, "I think, therefore I am." I was beginning to believe that, "I feel, therefore I have a soul." Just making that statement required me to use the word "believe." I couldn't prove it. I was beginning to recognize "belief" as another way of "knowing." Logic can only go so far. Pascal had also said, "The heart has its reasons of which reason knows nothing."[4] So many things that I formerly was unwilling to accept had now moved into the horizon of possibility. My last defenses against God were shattering, but I wasn't yet willing to throw in the towel. It would take another intervention by some unknown someone outside myself to push me beyond doubt into belief.

Carolyn and I had become committed to our marriage. That's different than simply becoming committed to stay married. We had done that, but had made an unpleasant discovery. Carolyn had always made the assumption that if I just didn't drink, everything would be all right. I hadn't had a drink in over a year, but everything certainly wasn't all right. Having made the decision to stay married, we had taken the possibility of trading the pain of a contentious marriage for the pain of divorce off the table. We were now faced with a choice: Either learn to live painfully with things as they were between us, or try to work on making things better. I figured attempting improvement was worth a try.

In the late 1970s, marriage enrichment retreats were in vogue. While many churches offered homegrown programs, a format developed in the Roman Catholic Church became extremely popular. Though developed in the Catholic

Church, it was open to people of other faiths or even no faith. "The weekend," as it was often called, consisted of husband and wife getting away to a hotel with a couple of dozen other couples where they were taught a communication tool called "the dialogue." The dialogue was a simple, but extremely powerful, idea. One of the facilitators would give a short talk on a topic. At the end of the talk, he or she would pose a question to the group. Then, without comment or any other conversation, each person would find a quiet place to be alone and would write an answer to the question during a prescribed-length time period. At the end of that time, the person would meet alone with his or her spouse and each would read aloud to the other the answer they had written to the question. There were rules in place to guide the conversation that followed—rules that, if followed, would result in the couple emotionally supporting one another and would prevent the emotional abuse that would have been brought on by derision or argument.

Carolyn and I had made it through a couple of short sessions on Friday night, the start of the retreat. By short, I mean ten to fifteen minutes of writing followed by a like period of sharing with each other. Saturday morning the sessions got progressively longer. We were now writing and sharing for twenty to thirty minutes in each dialogue exercise. After lunch on Saturday, the talk that was presented focused on self-identification as well as our roles and the associated expectations that came with them. We were told that this was the first of several major questions we would be given to dialogue on during the rest of the weekend. These major questions would have extended dialogue periods of one hour for writing followed by one hour for sharing our dialogue. The last question of the weekend would demand a full hour and a half each of writing and sharing. The question we were given to dialogue on that afternoon was simple to state, but potentially difficult to answer: Who are you?

I began forming answers to the question even as I walked to the place where I had chosen to write. Once ensconced in a comfortable chair, I gave another few minutes to think about an answer. I had been an English major in college. I had never been very good at writing outlines to guide my writing. But I had developed the practice of considering topics and themes and mentally jotting some notes before beginning any writing exercise. That approach left me open to wandering about in my writing to other thoughts that came to mind in the process—a practice that some readers find endearing and others find maddening. So I sat and began to organize my thoughts.

I was a husband. This was a marriage enrichment retreat, after all. That seemed like a good place to start. I was a father. I was a musician. Or at least, I had always wanted to be. I played several instruments. I loved jazz. But I had gotten married in my junior year of college and then had to work to support a family. That had left me feeling trapped. There went my hope for a career as a jazz musician. Anger and resentment started to build. Oops. Not exactly a productive path for a marriage enrichment dialogue. Besides, wasn't the real reason I wasn't making a living as a musician the reality that I had seldom practiced and usually used all music venues from rehearsals to gigs to live the "high life" of boozing as a hipster *poseur*? Self-pity began to well up. Oops. Also not exactly a productive path for a marriage enrichment dialogue. It would be better to save this stuff for A.A. inventory exercises and sharing with my sponsor.

Back to the mental outline drawing board. I am a husband. I am a father. I like to listen to and play jazz. I work

with computers. I am a churchgoer. I am an alcoholic.

After a few minutes a had a pretty good mental grasp on which elements of self I was going to write on, the order in which I'd address the topics, and what I wanted to say about each. I opened my notebook, picked up my pen, and without further thought promptly wrote, "I am a child of God." I stared at the sentence in disbelief and burst into tears. Nowhere had that thought arisen in my mental rehearsal of what I was going to write. It came, unbidden, out of the blue. I was surprised, startled, dumb-founded. Though mentally confused, I sensed a strange peace in my soul. There, I said I had a soul. I don't remember making a decision on the point. It just suddenly was no longer a question. The matter was settled.

The phenomenon I experienced is called "automatic writing." Many people consider the activity to be occult, akin to "channeling" or acting as a medium for spirits to communicate with humanity. I understand the concern this practice gives to people who profess faith in Christ and believe the injunctions of the Bible. I share those concerns when automatic writing is pursued and practiced as a means of revelation from people who are dead, one's "higher self," or God. I am more concerned about the first two than the third. I would admit that automatic writing is not normally a means for God's communication to and through people, but I don't think it can't be so. To use "God" and "can't" in the same sentence seems almost blasphemous. Like any revelation, the source can be judged from the content. This episode on a Saturday afternoon in 1977 was the only time I have experienced automatic writing—a means of communication I neither pursued nor pursue nor regularly practice. It just seems to me that if God could speak through fire (Dt 4.33), he can choose to use other non-normative mean to communicate if he chooses to do so. In fact, the Bib'

acknowledges that God speaks "in various ways." (He 1.1)

"I am a child of God." From where had that thought come? Was a Higher Power, The Great Warm Fuzzy, or God as I understand him breaking through my inability to make a decision by informing me that the decision had already been made and that now it was time to get on with accepting and living into it?

I used the last few minutes of the hour set aside for writing to scratch out a few thoughts on the roles that I had put on my mental list. I wasn't very eloquent in my writing or in my sharing that followed with Carolyn.

Something had happened. On the day I didn't kill myself, a realization or revelation that my life would never change, that my alcoholism would define my life for as long as I lived became an inarguable truth. That realization plunged me into despair so deep I couldn't remain there. The crises of despair propelled me into recovery. On the day I wrote, "I am a child of God," I realized that my life had changed. Someone had entered it in a way that had effected a transformation in my soul. That transformation would now define my life for as long as I lived. Surprise! Resistance would be futile.

∞

Coming Out

My life had certainly become much different in the fifteen months since I had my last drink. When I left home in the morning I had a pretty good idea of when I'd be home that evening. My home life had begun to develop some consistency. I still was going to seven or eight meetings a week. They fell into a recurring pattern from which I seldom deviated. The Sunday morning breakfast meeting that had been a cornerstone of my week for the first six months of sobriety had been replaced by church. Sunday night, Carolyn and I would still often go to an open speaker's meeting. Monday night was a men's stag meeting. Tuesday night was my home group, a co-ed closed meeting of forty to sixty alcoholics committed to recovery. Carolyn sometimes rode along on Tuesday nights since there was an Al-Anon meeting at the same facility on that night. Wednesday night was a Big Book study and Thursday night a step study. Friday night, Carolyn and I often went to an open speaker's meeting together and then out to coffee with folks—sort of a date night. Saturday I made a meeting at the Alano Club, either morning or afternoon depending on when I was running errands. Sometimes both. Or I'd go to an evening meeting if I hadn't been to one yet that day and was antsy. Once in a while, I'd go to all three if I were really white-knuckling it that day.

White-knuckle days were ones when I was fully incensed that people, places, or things were not conforming to my script for how things ought to be that day. Perhaps Carolyn had the temerity to ask me about something I was doing and I took her inquiry as a challenge to my autonomy, or it was hot and I was sweaty, or the lawn mower wouldn't start, or...whatever. Encountering almost any obstacle could set me off. One aspect of my defects of character was a proclivity to push when things were not going well rather than to stop and take a breath. "Easy Does It" hadn't made it off the slogan list and into my life as yet. If a nut were stuck going onto a bolt, I'd get a longer-handled wrench to force it on with more leverage. Of course, it was cross-threaded and I had just stripped the threads. That would make me furious: Stupid nut! Stupid bolt! Followed by: Stupid me! Slow down, step back, take a breath, think it through, put it aside for a while and come back to it later. None of these were options I naturally took.

But slowly, slowly, progress was made. I tried to be satisfied with the pace since we were told to seek progress rather than perfection.

The marriage retreat weekend had been my first attempt to let Carolyn into my inner-life. Like many people who carry an outward appearance of confidence and competence, my hollow insides were filled with fear that I'd be found out to be the scared little boy I felt like. To let people in would be to open myself to criticism or even ridicule. The Emperor would have no clothes. I was a living, breathing, walking example of Fr. John Powell's book title, *Why Am I Afraid To Tell You Who I Am?* The answer, in my case, was because if you knew who I was, you might not like me. Unlike Al Franken's *Saturday Night Live* character from the early 1990s, Stuart Smalley (who regularly affirmed, "I'm good enough, I'm smart enough, and doggone it, people like me."), my secret mantra was, "I'm not good enough, I'm not smart enough, and doggone it, not many people like me." So my fears, insecurities, uncertainties, and doubts stayed as well hidden as I could keep them.

My second exercise in opening myself to my family was to take us all to church camp for a week during the second summer of my recovery. There was a Christian camp in the mountains about an hour and a half drive from our house. While non-denominational, our denominational church had supplied board members, counselors, and campers to the camp for many years. It was planned to be a good time. Our kids were old enough that they would each be in separate camps: One themed as an Indian village and one as an old-time western dude ranch. We would get to see them on Wednesday afternoon when we would give them more money since (the staff warned us) they had probably already spent what we had given them for the whole week during the first three days. The rest of the time they would be cared for, instructed, and entertained while Carolyn and I would have a week of just being together. I guess I hadn't realized that being a church camp meant that we'd have a morning Bible study, late morning sessions on Christian marriage and family topics, and evening meetings that were the direct descendents of old-time camp meeting services. At least we had our afternoons free for swimming, sleeping, and snacking.

So up the mountain we went on a Sunday afternoon for a week of fun, fellowship, and food for both body and soul. Announcements after dinner on Sunday evening mentioned that for early risers, the camp cooks deep-fried fresh donuts each morning and brewed coffee to be available an hour and a half before breakfast formally started at eight A.M. I'm not normally an early riser, but I've never been one to miss fresh donuts, especially when the camp cook confirmed that my favorite varieties were always on the menu: crinkly buttermilk old-fashioneds and light-as-a-feather raised yeast donuts, both drenched with a simple syrup glaze that was so sweet it made your teeth hurt.

Six-thirty Monday morning I was up, dressed, and ready to head down from the cabin to the broad veranda of the dining room for my fresh coffee and donuts. The only problem was that Carolyn is (a) not a morning person, and (b) never ready to eat anything much before noon. After a half-hour battle of the wills, I finally gave up, left her to her sweet dreams, and stormed out of the cabin, loudly slamming the door as I departed. There were very few donuts left when I arrived at seven-fifteen. Now I was really mad at Carolyn. My favorites were gone. The coffee hadn't been plugged in for forty-five minutes and was growing coolish. How inconsiderate of her not to get up and come with me. I vowed to start earlier the next day.

Tuesday morning I was up at six, ready to do battle with the sleeping dragon. Wheedling, cajoling, begging, pleading, and threatening did no good. Six-thirty was rapidly approaching when I gave up, flung myself through the soon to be slamming screen door, and stomped down the hill. The coffee was hot and both of my favorite donuts were there. But it's hard to be happy when you're mad and donuts have a way of turning to lead in a belly that's churning with anger.

Wednesday morning, I was up and dressed by six-fifteen. I didn't say a word to Carolyn. In fact, I had said very little to her for the past twenty-four hours. Stubbornness had its consequences. I'd show her. I left without a word, but with the usual door slam just in case she had managed to stay asleep. I wanted her awake to let her think about the good time she was missing. Wednesday morning's coffee and donuts were garnished with resentment and pouting. Good Heavens! Didn't she realize the effort I was making for us to be together and there she was, sleeping her way through a potentially wonderful time together on the veranda, drinking coffee, and watching me eat donuts.

Thursday morning, I was up and ready to go. I even left the cabin without the usual door slam. I would rise above my disappointment and have a wonderful morning—alone. It actually was a pretty good morning. A soft summer breeze was wafting through the veranda. The coffee was hot and strong. The donuts were especially good, particularly when compared with the ones eaten in bitterness and resentment the prior three days. I enjoyed watching squirrels and Steller's jays chasing each other around the pines and live oak trees. The crowd was a little smaller that morning. Daily donut eating thins the ranks of those not truly committed to gastronomical excess. When I was ready to go back to the cabin at seven-thirty to escort sleeping beauty down to breakfast, there were still donuts left. In a flash, I had a brilliant idea. I would fix a cup of coffee the way Carolyn liked it, wrap a donut in a napkin, and take it up to the cabin to show her what she had been missing.

So it was that I was striding up the hill on a Thursday morning in the summer sunshine, coffee and donut in hand, smiling as I gleefully thought how bad Carolyn would feel when she saw how I had risen above her petty obstinacy and was magnanimously going to present her with a treat, when I heard a voice call out from the cabin where our family relationship teacher and his wife were staying for the week. "Loving your wife, I see," he said. I almost stumbled when it hit me. I wasn't loving Carolyn at all. Once again, I had decided what would be best and was trying to force everyone into my scheme of things whether they wanted to participate or not. It stung all the more because I was being commended for what appeared to be a loving action when, in fact, my motive was contemptible. Busted. Greatly chagrined, I presented Carolyn with my offerings. Humiliation must have passed for humility because she seemed really touched that I had let her sleep in, thought of her, and brought her a gift. Sometimes grace abounds when least expected and certainly not deserved. Maybe that's the whole point of grace.

I'm sure the week's teachings were interesting and helpful. I'm always interested in learning new things. I can't catalogue the insights gained or knowledge acquired. Understanding creeps in line upon line, precept upon precept, or so it's said. Friday evening came and the week was almost over. The message that night was highly evangelistic. Somehow, my cynicism was turned off. I just listened without the internal debate that usually interacts with what I'm hearing any speaker say. Things just seemed to make sense. I had the strangest sensation. The speaker would say something and my internal response was, "I know that." Not, "I get that," or "That makes sense to me," but rather "I already know that," even though if you'd have asked me a few seconds before I heard the speaker say it, I couldn't have verbalized what I now was sure I knew. The word that comes to mind to describe the phenomenon is "assurance." I had an assurance that what I was hearing was not only true, but that I had known it for a long time.

At the end of the message, the speaker gave the rather standard Evangelical Christian "invitation:" While every head is bowed and every eye is closed; raise your hand if you want to receive Jesus as Lord and Savior. I didn't respond. It wasn't fear or embarrassment that prevented me. I just didn't think I met the criterion. I didn't need to receive Christ. I felt like I already had. Sometime in the fifteen month period between not killing myself and realizing "I am a child of God," I had to have received Christ. I had heard that "to all who received him, to those who believed in his name, he gave the right to become children of God." (Jn 1.12) If I was a child of God, I had to have received him and believed in his name. The old saying goes, "The proof of the pudding is in the eating." If I was so and so, I had to have done such and such. Was it a problem that I couldn't remember when? Did I have to do something else to become something I already felt I was? It didn't feel right.

The speaker then went on to situation number two. If you had once received Christ and walked away and wanted to re-dedicate yourself to Jesus as Lord and savior, with every head bowed and every eye closed, raise your hand. Again, I didn't raise my hand. I didn't think I met that criterion either. Had I received Christ and believed in[1] him and then walked away? I had no recollection of either.

The speaker then went on to his final invitation. If you had received Christ, but had never publicly acknowledged that fact and wanted to do so, raise your hand. Got me. That was me to a tee. I looked at the speaker, raised my hand, and then discovered that every head wasn't bowed and every eye wasn't closed. A woman from our church was looking at me and smiling. Busted. I was no longer undeclared. I had "come out," so to speak. I was now a publicly professing disciple of Jesus the Christ of God, an apprentice to the master, a follower of someone other than myself. I was a professing Christian.

∞

| 12 |
Surprised Again

Fast forward with me to 1985. I had been clean and sober for nine years. I had come to faith. My marriage was committed and growing. My children were in college or about to graduate from high school. We had stayed together as a family. In lighter moments we'd say we had been happily married for nine years, although the wedding had been twenty-one years ago. Gallows humor seems to be strangely comforting to people who have been through trauma and brokenness. We were on the path to wholeness—on the path, but not yet whole.

I sometimes wonder if anyone ever really does become whole in this life. The Apostle Paul uses a rich metaphor when he writes, "Now we see a poor reflection as in a mirror; then we shall see face to face. Now I know in part; then I shall know fully, even as I am fully known." (1Co 13.12) In this life, our brokenness will always prevent our seeing fully and knowing fully. The key to the good life is not to attain perfection without brokenness, but rather to find a path through our brokenness that enables us to enjoy life with God while avoiding doing harm to others and ourselves. Our path begins with acknowledgment, continues with honesty, but doesn't go very far unless we embrace the value of others at a foundational level.

Paul says in another place, "we who have this spiritual treasure are like common pots of clay to show that the supreme power belongs to God, not to us." (2Co 4.7 GNT) Clay pots are fired to make them hard and strong. But their hardness and strength also makes them brittle and therefore fragile. Fired clay pots are subject to cracks—brokenness if you will. Perhaps the best description of the human condition is that we're all cracked pots. But when we're filled with the treasure of God indwelling us, we are somehow miraculously held together. Through the cracks we can see the source of our strength, the hidden treasure that is God. A friend once said she finds broken people more authentic than people who are seemingly all together because the brokenness allows her to see through to the person's soul.

The brokenness that defeats us is that which we disguise and hide. We act as if it did not exist in an attempt to appear strong. Rather, our disingenuousness is our downfall. Without honesty, disclosure, and cooperation with God to seal the cracks in our clay pots, we disintegrate into dysfunction and despair. The trick is to find that harmony wherein one can embrace the pain, trust the process, judge oneself neither too softly nor too harshly, and surrender our brokenness to the one who will give us the good life of *shalom* by his embrace of our authentic self. In that embrace we are fully known and loved unconditionally. We're always loved unconditionally, but we lack the ability to make brokenness bearable until we're able to receive and accept that love. When we enter that harmony of brokenness and wholeness we can live out the paradox that Paul describes: "We are hard pressed on every side, but not crushed; perplexed, but not in despair; persecuted, but not abandoned; struck down, but not destroyed." (2Co 4.8-9) We become a strange people, acknowledging our brokenness but able somehow to live at peace, content without being complacent, always working toward wholeness but never striving, knowing that we'll never attain complete wholeness in this life. Yet living in the sure and certain hope that one-day when we see Christ face to face "we will be like him." (1Jn 3.3)

This is not the place to dwell in depth on progress along the path during the eight years that followed the fifteen months that comprise the setting for the part of my story that is the subject of this book. Perhaps one day I'll tell that part of my story. But an incident that defined the end of that second portion of my story is a fitting capstone for this portion.

By 1985, Carolyn and I had left the traditional denominational church that was part of this first phase of my story. We didn't leave because we were mad or disappointed. We had learned so much at that church about the Bible and a life of discipleship. We will always be grateful for our time there.

I had sensed a call to enter vocational ministry. Age forty with one child in college and one at home in high school did not seem like an auspicious time to start a seminary process that would lead to denominational ordination. Besides, I had come under the influence of the Charismatic Renewal and had vision for a more organic process of establishing and leading churches than that used by the denomination of which we were a part. We became part of the flagship church of a non-denominational movement that focused on evangelism and church planting. We had attended a rigorous two-year church planting school at the church. The night had come when, following the practice of our movement, the leaders of the church would lay hands on us and commission us to relocate and start a new church.

Everything had flowed as expected. The service began with about forty-five minutes of worship music followed by announcements during which the offering was taken. Carolyn and I were called to the platform, the leaders gathered around us, laid hands on us, prayed for God to anoint us with every gift needed for our new vocation, commissioned us to the task of church planting, and released us from the congregation we had called home for five years. Our pastor preached a sermon. Typically, the sermon was followed with what we called ministry time. The pastor would usually call the band and singers back to the platform and invite people to come forward for prayer. Often he would announce specific areas for which he sensed some in the meeting needed prayer. During that time, people would come forward for prayer while the band continued to lead the congregation in singing additional worship songs while the ministry was going on.

That night was different. It was not unique, for what transpired had happened before on occasion, but rarely. The pastor hadn't invited either the band to the platform or people in the congregation to come forward for prayer. On these rare occasions, the pastor would go to the piano and play and quietly sing an old hymn or gospel song while he waited to sense from God what he was to do next. I always enjoyed the times when that happened. There seemed to be a quiet reverence that would fall over the church while we all waited on a sense of direction from God. That night he began to softly sing and play an old gospel song:

> Have Thine own way, Lord. Have Thine own way.
>   Thou art the Potter, I am the clay.
> Mold me and make me after Thy will,
>   While I am waiting, yielded and still.[1]

I stood transfixed. I knew that song. Like the taste of a madeleine and tea that transported Swann's memory involuntarily to an incident at Combray in Proust's *Remembrance of Things Past*, that song engaged my memory and transported me to a time in my childhood. I was eight years old. I often spent extended stays during summers with my cousins on a farm in rural, upstate Pennsylvania. My aunt was the organist at a Methodist-Episcopal church in the little town that served as the county seat.

During that summer's stay, the church hosted a Vacation Bible School. My aunt taught one of the VBS classes and played the organ for the children's service that closed each morning's meeting. At each of these closing services, the superintendent of the Vacation Bible School would ask if anyone had prayed for forgiveness of their sins and invited Jesus into their heart that morning. If so, the person was to come forward to be acknowledged as a new Christian. The practice then was for the new Christian to recite a Bible verse that had prompted him or her to take such a momentous step.

It was the second to the last day of VBS. The superintendent asked the usual question and I rose and went forward. I had prayed for forgiveness of sin that morning and invited Jesus into my heart. When asked what Bible verse I wanted to recite, however, I said that it wasn't a Bible verse that had stirred me that week. I asked if, as my testimony, I could sing a song that we had sung several times that week: One that had stirred my young soul, led me to contemplation of eternity, and prompted a choice as to how I wanted to live my life. In what was, I'm sure, a trembling, high-pitched voice, I began singing, "Have Thine own way, Lord. Have Thine own way...."

That night in 1985 as I heard that song sung and the memory of my childhood profession of faith came unbidden to mind, I thought I heard God whisper, "I've known you since you were eight years old." I reflected on that moment several times over the next few days. I couldn't shake one nagging question: What would have happened to me if I had died while I thought I was an atheist? Silly, isn't it? I think God would simply have had his way with me. But really, that's what always happens anyway, isn't it? Arminian Protestantism asserts we have a choice regarding acceptance of God's invitation based on our own free will. Yet in a parable of a great feast—the feast usually is interpreted as symbolizing eternal relationship in fellowship with God—when those invited to the feast rejected the invitation, the master tells his servants to "Go out into the roads and lanes, and compel people to come in." (Lk 14:23 NRSV) *Compel them.* In a strange way, "God's compulsion is our liberation."[2]

God had known me since I was eight. I had spent the last eight years growing in the grace of knowing him. Had I been a believer all along? Can we believe things at a level beneath our conscious thoughts? I don't know. Like so many things, I simply put it in the big bucket of mystery that is perhaps the best description of what relating to God is like.

What I do know is this: There is a grace by which I stand. (Ro 5.2) That grace infused me when I made promises and invitations beyond my childhood ability to understand. God seems to have taken those promises and invitations much more seriously than I did for most of my adolescence and early adult life. I had come from faithlessness to faith. I was learning to live in the simplicity-complexity of not knowing beyond doubt but believing, nevertheless, that someone who desires my good is in control and learning to trust that belief. Had this journey been of my devising or God's? Did it matter? Once again, words from the pen of Paul seem to capture the kernel of what I understand. "But by the grace of God I am what I am, and his grace to me as not without effect. No, I worked harder than all of them—yet not I, but the grace of God that was with me." (1Co 15.10) I am learning to live and trust in the uncomfortable comfort of knowing that "The one who calls [me] is faithful and he will do it." (1Th 5.24)

∞

| Epilogue |
Happy, Joyous, and Free

It seems fitting to end this story of "what happened," as The Big Book would say, by briefly exploring the state of "what I'm like now." My ongoing story of recovery and redemption has brought me to a state characterized by the phrase that prompted a key turning point in my journey. I am living a life that is "happy, joyous, and free."

Along the way, I discovered that the journey that began as a search for sobriety could not continue without a spiritual awakening. I certainly didn't begin my journey looking for a spiritual awakening, but I found one or, perhaps, one found me. In fact, one of the titles I considered for this book was *I Once Was Found*—a parody of a line in the hymn *Amazing Grace*: "I once was lost."[1] I've come to realize that often more is planned for each of us than we plan for ourselves.

A.A. emphasizes the indispensible role of a spiritual awakening in the process of recovery by beginning the Twelfth Step with the phrase "Having had a spiritual awakening as a result of these steps." Having a spiritual awakening is a forgone conclusion for those who attain serenity as well as sobriety by following the Twelve Steps of A.A.'s program of recovery. A spiritual awakening, therefore, is a goal as well as a means to a goal.

"Having had a spiritual awakening as a result of these steps" I have continued to "trudge the Road of Happy Destiny"[2] (as the A.A. Big Book so flamboyantly puts it) toward serenity and sobriety one day at a time for the past thirty-five years. Like the lives of everyone else I know, some days are better than others. I'm not sure I even believe the old A.A. adage, "My worst day sober is better than my best day drunk." But while we live one day at a time, a person assesses his or her life over a period of time. Somewhere along the way, I began to form a new outlook regarding my life. I began to live into the promise of a life that was happy, joyous, and free.

At first blush, the words "happy" and "joyous" may appear redundant. But the two are quite different. There are, to my way of thinking, two primary differences. Both differences are in regard to time. In the first regard, happiness is very much a matter of the present. It is a pleasant feeling of satisfaction and contentment. It lurks under the surface of life and beneath the level of consciousness. It isn't revealed until you ask yourself the question, "Am I happy?" or "What am I feeling?" To accept the distinction made by Samuel Alexander,[3] happiness is an experience I enjoy but of which I am unaware until I contemplate or assess the state of my life in the present.

Joy also ambushes us from beneath the level of our awareness. My primary influence in understanding the anatomy of joy is C. S. Lewis' *Surprised By Joy*. Lewis uses the word "surprised" in two ways.* First, at the end of his journey of

---

* Two years after *Surprised By Joy* was written, a third meaning that could not have been anticipated became appropriate. Lewis, a life-long bachelor until age fifty-eight, met and married a woman named Joy

conversion, he is surprised by the role played in the process by something he has come to call "Joy." Second—and this is the sense in which I am now addressing it—joy always arrives unexpectedly. A common phrase used by Lewis refers to it as a "stab of Joy." I've described it in my own experience as suddenly "feeling big"—not like Gulliver among the Lilliputians big, but suddenly bigger than life. Joy pierces our unsuspecting present with "a thrill," "a fluttering of the diaphragm" that leaves us "sick with desire; that sickness better than health."[4] Joy always is experienced as a moment of ecstasy, but it simultaneously contains an element of longing for something that is not yet, for something seeming close enough to touch but remaining too far away to grasp. It is the delicious tingling of living in anticipation of something good, wonderful, and delightful drawing close—not yet seen, but being almost palpable in its presence.

Both happiness and joy, then, are experiences in the present. We are unaware of our current state of happiness until we are caused to reflect on and define our current state. We are unaware that joy lurks just below the surface of our consciousness until it erupts, stabs us with a thrill, and transports us beyond the here and now to a place it seems we've never been, yet that feels undeniably like home, the place we were meant to be.

The second way in which time plays a role in my understanding of happiness and joy has to do with duration. Happiness can be a sensation that is seen as covering a period of time. That period may be a season of our life or our entire life. But whether a season or in entirety, the key is that the sensation is perceived when we retrospectively view either the period or the whole of our life to date. An assessment of one's life as "happy" need not mean that every day or every

---

Greshem. Their romance was given a fictionalized treatment first as a play entitled *Shadowlands* and then in a film of the same name.

period of life has been filled with happiness. But the prevailing tenor of one's life is deemed to be happy by the only one whose overall assessment matters—the one who has lived it.

Were I to seek a synonym for this overarching happiness that may characterize a period of time, I could do no better than the ancient Hebrew word *shalom*. Those who prepare glosses for quick translations of foreign words have done us a disservice by stating that *shalom* means "peace." It is so much more than that. Its basic meaning is not the narrow sense of "peace," as in lack of relational hostility (although *shalom* certainly includes peace without relational hostility) but rather the broader sense of "wellbeing." It implies stability, contentment, and satisfaction. It includes a connotation of covenant—a unilateral declaration by God that his intent toward his creation is for goodness to befall it rather than harm. (Je 29.11)

Happiness, therefore, applies to an indefinite period. It characterizes a season even if it doesn't fill it. Because happiness is an assessment of a period, it is always seen in our rearview mirror rather than through our windshield. We assess happiness as we look back over time at our state of being during an interval. There is, then, a sense of flow, of continuance, of duration to happiness that is not found in joy. Joy is punctiliar. It occurs at a point in time. It punctures our present in a way that Lewis describes as a "stab." While it occurs in the "here and now" it always contains a hint of anticipation of something just out of reach or just out of view. One of the best artistic portrayals of this type of joy, for me, is the song "Something's Coming," in *West Side Story*.[5] Phrases in the lyrics evoke appearances of phenomena in ways so sudden and unexpected that the character Tony is almost transported outside himself with anticipation. The song is punctuated with sharp, *staccato*, syncopated rhythms that explosively interject chords in a way that causes the hearer to feel the "stab of Joy" viscerally. To experience what I mean, find a recording of the song either by the original cast or the movie soundtrack and play it at chest-thumping volume. Then apologize to your neighbors for the disturbance.

If we can differentiate between happiness and joy, then, we can find the difference between being happy and joyous. Being happy is being in a state of pleasant, satisfied, contentment produced by events and interactions over a period of time. That period may be as brief as a few hours or as long as a lifetime. Being joyous is a state verging on the ecstatic in which one is ambushed by stabs of joy that overwhelm one. These moments are rightly described as joyous. But can the word joyous be appropriately assigned to the other moments of a person's life? I contend that one can live in a state that leaves one susceptible to the possibility of being ambushed by moments of joy. I would use the word joyous to describe not only the moments when joy overtakes us but also to describe a state of being in which it is possible for those moments of joy to overtake us, i.e., one may be joyous without experiencing the thrill of joy at the moment. The question begs to be asked, can we enable ourselves to become happy and joyous through conscious actions?

The first question is how can a person effectively pursue happiness. Here we enter the realm of paradox. The sad truth is that happiness is least likely to be obtained by its pursuit. In an article in *Psychology Today* read so many decades ago that I have no hope of retrieving a citation, the author(s) of the article showed, based on their research, that those who placed higher value on living in ways of benefit to others were more likely to be happy than those whose stated goal was the attainment of their own happiness. By this evaluation, happiness appears to be a byproduct of a life well and even altruistically lived rather than the end product of a life dedicated to its pursuit and attainment. The best way to pursue happiness, therefore, seems to be to be less concerned with one's own happiness than with the happiness of others.

The new attitude being formed in my life by the twin influences of A.A.'s program of recovery and my spiritual awakening that was manifest as a religious conversion led me to a consideration of others that I had not had heretofore. Both A.A.'s concept of service and Jesus' exhortation to love my neighbor provided impetus to what I describe with the coined word "otherliness." This focus on otherliness provides the antidote to the narcissism inherent in addiction. It leads to the prospect of happiness arriving as a byproduct of a life well led

I think that happiness of this sort requires appreciation of both our state of existence and those elements that have produced it. For me, the foundation for all that makes for happiness or *shalom* as a state of being is a God who holds a gracious intent toward me, and not only me, but also toward all creation. The most elemental way that that gracious intent can be described is by saying that God loves me. My happiness lives in the sense of security that nothing can separate me from that love.

The second question is how can one effectively pursue joy. This appears at first glance to be more difficult because joy erupts in us in unanticipated moments. The possibility that joy may puncture the commonplace from time to time requires that I live in a state of hope. Hope is the field in which joy may erupt. As such, hope may be considered as a synonym for the state of being I am calling "joyous"—the state which may be pierced by stabs of joy. By introducing the word "hope" I am adding a key element to the discussion for consideration.

"Hope" is, perhaps, a more often used and more easily understood concept than the state of being I have labeled as "joyous." It is a state of living in anticipation of something good coming to be. Such hope is an essential component of Christian faith.[6] It refuses to believe that "the world ends not with a bang but a whimper"[7] and declares that the consummation of God's plan and purpose will be announced with a shout of triumph and celebration.

When I write that to experience joy one must live in hope, "in" is an important word. The requisite kind of hope is "hope in" rather than "hope for." "Hope in" is the hope referred to in the trilogy of "faith, hope and love" identified as things that endure, remain, or abide. (1Co 13.13) "Hope for" places my anticipation of joy into something I can define, describe, or envision. Since I can define, describe, or envision it, it lacks the dimension of surprise that the experience of joy brings. Surprise or unexpectedness, however, is an essential element of joy. "Hope for" runs the risk of the thing or situation being hoped for not being obtained or happening. What then follow are disappointment, regret, and dissatisfaction—hardly elements conducive to *shalom*.

"Hope in" is biblical hope and always refers to a person. One may object that people often disappoint us as well. "Hope in" only opens the door to the possibility of joy if the one hoped in can be trusted. Trust, here, is a simple synonym for "faith." I have discovered that the one to have hope in, to trust in, to have faith in, is God. A.A. says it this way, "Without help it is too much for us. But there is One who has all power—that One is God."[8] The Bible says it this way, "God is love. (1Jn 4.16) ... Love never fails. (1Co 13.8) ... The one who calls you is faithful and he will do it." (1Th 5.24)[9]

To have hope requires a conscious renunciation of pessimism. This renunciation is not a Pollyannaish optimism that lives in the denial of evil or the delusion that all will always be well. It is to answer "yes" to Einstein's alleged question, "Is the universe a friendly place?" Answering "yes" breeds hope just as answering "no" breeds fear. Fear produces a posture of protection and defensiveness in which we cannot live unguardedly. But it is only in unguarded moments that the stab of joy can thrill our hearts. To live defensively denies one the possibility of experiencing joy. Experiencing joy requires us to accept risk. As Helen Keller once said:

> Security is mostly a superstition. It does not exist in nature, nor do the children of men as a whole experience it. Avoiding danger is no safer in the long run than outright exposure. Life is either a daring adventure, or nothing.[10]

Admittedly, it is hard to risk in the face of fear. Since "There is no fear in love. [and] perfect love drives out fear," (1Jn 4:18) receiving, experiencing, and trusting in the perfect love that comes from God alone are keys to facing fear, taking the risk of deciding that the universe is a friendly place (which is another way of saying that God is friendly, i.e., has a gracious intent toward us), and thereby living in a joyous state—a state of hope—that is susceptible to being pierced from time to time by stabs of joy.

I know I'm heading for trouble if my state of being starts to shift from hope toward fear. For me, that's the signal to step back, evaluate what's going on and where I've departed from the manner of living I've been given as a gift, and return to reliance on God and his love. The realization of the centrality of this process to my continued sobriety and serenity was brought home to me by an event that occurred almost twenty years ago. I had disclosed to my board that I had begun to spiral downward toward depression. A very discerning, prayerful, and godly woman on the board began to pray both for me and for understanding from God as to how she might be helpful to me. She came to me a few weeks later. She said that she had received a strong, recurring impression that she was to come to me and tell me that Zechariah 9:12 was the Lord's counsel to me to understand both the source of my distress and the solution for it.

Zechariah 9:12 says, "Return to your fortress, O prisoners of hope; even now I announce that I will restore twice as much to you." I immediately knew what this meant. Sixteen times the psalmists refer to God as their fortress. My fortress is to be God and his love for me. Placing my trust anywhere else is leaving my fortress. If I return to deep and abiding trust in him, I will continue to live into an ever-increasing sense of *shalom*. At that moment I seemed to hear the phrase, "My heart is held captive by hope." That's now who I now understand myself to be: A prisoner of hope.

I have come to generally characterize my life as happy. I consider it joyous because my affirmation of the friendliness of the universe has dispelled fear and left me open to the possibility of being surprised by joy. I live with my heart captive to hope instead of fear. I don't want to imply that my release from fear was a simple matter of choice—a positive affirmation, if you will. Most transitions are gradual rather than cataclysmic, processes rather than events. Pickles are made by sealing cucumbers in a jar filled with a brine and acid solution. If natural fermentation is relied on provide the acid, the pickling process takes six to eight weeks. Opening the jar of pickles prematurely provides only salty cucumbers. The transformation from cucumbers to pickles occurs slowly through the course of the pickling process. So it has been with many transitions in my life. Sometimes, however, an event seems to accelerate or confirm a process in a way that makes the transformation appear as an event rather than a process. So it was with the dismissal of the pervasive sense of fear from my life that had caused me to live with a sense of dread and foreboding for as long as I can remember.

Approaching my fourth year of sobriety, life became very difficult. I had left a large corporation the prior year after thirteen years of prosperous employment. Since then I had participated in two business start-ups that foundered. Carolyn and I survived by taking first a second and then a third mortgage on our house. Finally, I divested myself of entrepreneurial dreams and found employment at a stable company. The wolf was no longer at the door, but I lived in fear. When I picked up my message slips at work, if I saw a name I didn't recognize I was sure that it was an attorney notifying me of a lawsuit on behalf of a creditor or disgruntled customer. When the phone would ring, my heart would immediately begin to pound and the thought that sized my mind was that someone was calling to tell me my children were dead. I was not in a good space.

About this time, we had reconnected with my wife's former sister-in-law whom we hadn't seen since her divorce from my brother-in-law several years before. During the time we were out of touch, she had also had a conversion and become a follower of Jesus. We went to a birthday party being held in her honor. We arrived almost at the stated time for ending the gathering. I expressed disappointment that we would miss spending time with her. She graciously refrained from pointing out that that wouldn't have happened had I been on time. Her conversion certainly had mellowed her. "But," she said, "if you want to spend time with me, come to church and we'll go get a bite to eat afterward." Mostly her new church friends attended the party and they were about to leave for a Sunday evening service. I had heard of her church as one of the "new churches" or so-called "Third Wave Churches." I was interested in seeing what the church was like as well as in spending more time with her, so we went.

The service was simple and unpretentious. It was held in a high school gym. The musical portion of worship was led by a folk-rock-pop-influenced band complete with a competent rhythm section and background vocalists to support the lead singer. The atmosphere was casual. Everyone was dressed in Southern California Sunday afternoon chic. Shorts, Hawaiian shirts, and sandals seemed to be the dress code. What impressed me most was the sense of adoration that could be perceived as the congregation sang love songs to Jesus rather than hymns about him. As a musician, my musical tastes were pleasantly satisfied.

The speaker that night—not the regular pastor—began meandering his way through a text with frequent backtrackings and restatements. Abruptly he closed his Bible and said, "The Lord won't let me continue ("Thanks be to God," I thought). He's telling me he wants to do some healing tonight." At this, my ears pricked up. Prayer for healing was one of the practices that had caused me to have some interest in this particular church. "The first thing he wants to do," the speaker announced, "is to set three men free who are debilitated by fear. The Lord says that if they'll just stand, he'll deliver them." First one man and then another stood. Small cohorts of people gathered around them to pray for them to be released from the debilitating grip of fear. I waited and watched for the third man to stand. Though not antagonistic to the new churches, I was, nevertheless, skeptical of some of the stories I had heard.

After a pause, the speaker said, "The Lord's telling me there are three men to be prayed for. He won't release me to go on until the third one stands." After an embarrassing silence he said, almost apologetically, "We really don't do things this way. We don't believe in coercion or manipulation, but the Lord's telling me this guy doesn't know it's him we're waiting on."

Suddenly, I knew it was me. I was the third man who was debilitated by fear. The realization so startled me that I involuntarily started forward in my chair. Almost as if something or someone else took over, the motion continued slowly as if the momentum of my initial movement was propelling me upward until I stood up fully. At the moment I was completely standing, I began to experience a strange sensation. At the same pace at which I had completed the standing motion, something began to roll up from my toes, progressed over my entire body, and left the top of my head. The sensation brought the thought to my mind that that's what it would feel like to a hand to have a doctor rolling a tight fitting surgical glove off of his or her hand. At the moment I felt something leave the top of my head, the speaker (who was fifty to sixty feet away from me) said, "That's it. You've been delivered from a spirit of fear." By then, people were gathering around me to pray, but the work, whatever it was, had already been done.

This event served as the catalyst in the process of my being released from a fear that at least inhibits if not prevents joy. From that time forward, I've never been gripped again by life-denying fear. I've been joyous, i.e., living in a state of being wherein it is possible to be surprised by joy at any moment. I had become free from fear.

Being free seems to be an important value in God's economy. As Jesus said, "If you hold to my teaching...you will know the truth, and the truth will set you free. ... If the Son sets you free, you will be free indeed." (Jn 8.31-36) Paul, in fact, affirms that "It is for freedom that Christ has set us free." (Ga 5.1) In another place he makes reference to the desirability of freedom by writing "I will not be mastered by anything." (1Co 6.12)

Freedom from the unholy trinity of addiction—a compulsion of the body coupled with an obsession of the mind and a malady of the spirit—comes almost paradoxically. When I was drinking, I thought I could stop but I couldn't. Then, when I surrendered to the reality that I couldn't stop drinking, I could stop. When I thought surrender to God would make me simply a pawn in his game, I couldn't surrender to him. But when I surrendered my will and my life to him, I became free in a way I didn't know was possible. The word "I" may set the wrong tone. As Paul writes, "I worked harder than any...though it was not I, but the grace of God that is with me." (1Co 15.10) Recovery and relationship with God have this in common: we don't earn either of them, but not earning something does not mean that no effort is required to obtain it. So I live in a freedom that was and is freely given but is not free from effort to attain and maintain.

The funny thing about freedom in the way I am writing about it is that it comes to be recognized as having already been found rather than being a goal that one can watch drawing ever closer until it is obtained. One simply recognizes after the fact that it is the state in which one is now living rather than knowing exactly when the entry into that state occurred. In this it is similar to my understanding of my conversion from being an uncaring agnostic to being a person of faith. I became aware that it had happened rather than that it was happening. That awareness comes with a sense of empowerment fueled by the recognition that something that once controlled you no longer does.

One way to describe this change of state would be to call it being born again. Just as a person does not remember his or her birth, so the second birth that brings new life is sometimes recognized as having happened even though it is not remembered. I don't think this "born again" reality is necessarily the same thing as the "born again" experience that Evangelical Christians equate with salvation. I don't think that it is required of everyone in order to be in right relationship with God. I just happen to be one of those to whom William James refers as the "twice born" in *The Varieties of Religious Experience*.[11] "Once born" people enter life with the belief that the universe is friendly. "Twice born" people are those who must make a transition to that belief. To classify the difference as simply an optimistic versus pessimistic outlook is both too simple and yet does capture something of the nature of the distinction. The phenomenon of being "twice born" is perhaps accurately described as being converted.

So, to put a point on the end of this story of recovery and redemption, I am a person who is happy, joyous, and free. My heart has been captured and held captive by hope. I am a prisoner of hope. My life still has its ups and downs. But viewed from this point in my life experiences, I see a *shalom* that I did not think possible through the first thirty-three years of living it. There has been a shift—a conversion at depth, if you will—in my basic understanding of the nature of life and its purpose. That shift has left me open to the ever-present hope of being surprised by joy. The result has been living in a freedom I not only did not think was possible for me, but could not even conceptualize as possible for anyone.

My hope is that if you are one who lives enslaved to a distressed life characterized by war with a hostile universe that this story will excite hope within you that you have a story with a similar arc to be lived. May that excitement be experienced as a stab of joy. I hope we will meet some day as we each "trudge the Road of Happy Destiny" so that you will have the opportunity to tell me your story. Thanks for listening to mine.

Shalom.

∞

| Endnotes |

| Prologue | Why Tell This Story?

1. Anonymous, *Alcoholics Anonymous: The Story of How Many Thousands of Men and Women Have Recovered from Alcoholism*, 4th ed. (New York: Alcoholics Anonymous World Services, 2001), xxiv.

2. Edward Grinnan, "My Faith: How storytelling saved my life," CNN, http://religion.blogs.cnn.com/2011/08/07/my-faith-how-storytelling-saved-my-life/?hpt=hp_c2 (accessed August 11, 2011).

3. Ibid.

4. I acknowledge indebtedness to the title of a book by Parker Palmer as the source of this phrase.

5. Anonymous, *Alcoholics Anonymous: The Story of How Many Thousands of Men and Women Have Recovered from Alcoholism*, 2nd ed. (New York: Alcoholics Anonymous World Services, 2001), 59.

6. Ibid., 58.

7. To explore the "outsider" ethos that keeps many people outside of the church, see Jim Henderson, Todd Hunter, and Greg Spinks, *The Outsider Interviews* (Grand Rapids: Baker Books, 2010).

8. J.B. Phillips, *Your God Is Too Small*, (New York: Macmillan, 1953).

9. Anonymous, *Twelve Steps and Twelve Traditions*, (New York: Alcoholics Anonymous Publishing, 1953), 12.

10. Ibid., 192.

11. Ibid., 9.

12. Ibid., 192.

| 1 | To Be or Not

1. Allen Ginsberg, *Howl, and Other Poems*, The Pocket Poets Series, No. 4 (San Francisco: City Lights Pocket Bookshop, 1956), lines 1-4.

2. Lawrence Durrell, *Balthazar: A Novel*, (New York: Dutton, 1958), 24.

3. Mark Twain, *The Adventures of Tom Sawyer* (Colorado Springs: Picadilly Books, 2010), 77.

4. D. Drew Pinsky, CNN, http://www.cnn.com/2011/OPINION/06/07/drew.pinsky.weiner/index.html?hpt=hp_bn9 (accessed June 7, 2011).

5. The verb form *metanoéō* is the present tense, active voice, command (imperative) form of the verb.

6. Anonymous, *Alcoholics Anonymous*, 2nd ed., 59.

| 3 | Honesty

1. Anonymous, *Alcoholics Anonymous*, 2nd ed., 58.

2. M. Scott Peck, *People of the Lie: The Hope for Healing Human Evil* (New York, Simon and Schuster, 1983).

| 4 |Humility

1. Bruce Springsteen, "Hungry Heart," (ASCAP, 1980).

2. Gregory Boyd, *The Myth of a Christian Religion* (Grand Rapids: Zondervan, 2009), 37.

3. Anonymous, *Twelve Steps and Twelve Traditions*, 99.

| 5 | Willing To Try Again

1. Anonymous, *Alcoholics Anonymous*, 2nd ed., 570. The Big Book attributes this quote to Herbert Spencer as do many quotation source books. However, Michael StGeorge has published an internet article at http://anonpress.org/spencer/ that documents his research that the quote in the above form was a restatement by Rev. William Poole of a quote from William Paley found on page 372 in a new edition of his complete works issued in one volume: *Complete Works of William Paley*. Philadelphia, PA: Crissy & Markley, 1850. Pool's restatement was placed on the title page of his book: William Poole. *Anglo-Israel*. Toronto: Bengough Bro.'s, 1879.

2. Ibid., 45.

3. Ibid. 59.

| 6 | Commitment

1. William Shakespeare, "Hamlet," http://shakespeare.mit.edu/ http://shakespeare.mit.edu/hamlet/full.html (accessed October 23 2011). Act III, scene 1, lines 70-71.

2. "Do You Love Me?," in *Fiddler on the Roof.* Music: Jerry Bock. Lyric: Sheldon Hamick. (1964).

3. George Santayana, *The Life of Reason*, vol. 1: Reason in Common Sense (New York: Scribner's, 1905), 284.

4. Anonymous, *Alcoholics Anonymous*, 2nd ed., 569.

| 8 | The Great Warm Fuzzy

1. Hazelden Foundation., *Twenty-Four Hours a Day*, Revised ed. (City Center, MI w: Hazelden, 1975).

2. Ibid., s.v. "January 1."

3. Santayana, *The Life of Reason*, 284.

4. Anonymous, *Alcoholics Anonymous*, 2nd ed., 60.

5. C. S. Lewis, *Surprised By Joy: The Shape of My Early Life* (Orlando: Harcourt Brace & Company, 1955), 173.

6. Ibid., 191.

7. Clara M. Brooks, "What a Mighty God We Serve!" (Public Domain, 1907).

| 9 | Because That's Just The Way It Is

1. Earl Thompson, *A Garden of Sand* (New York: Carroll & Graf, 2001).

2. William Shakespeare, "Hamlet." Act III, scene 1, lines 4-5.

3. Kahil Gibran, "The Madman," in *Spiritual World* (Guildford, UK: White Crow Books, 2009), 104.

4. Lewis, *Surprised By Joy, 229.*

5. Edward Rowland Sill, "An Adage from the Orient," in *Poetical Works* (New York: Houghton, Mifflin, 1906), 320.

6. George MacDonald, *Unspoken Sermons, Vol. 1, 2, & 3*, The Sunrise Centenary Editions of the Works of George MacDonald Sermons (Eureka: Sunrise Books Publishers, 2004), 260.

| 10 | Surprise!

1. Blaise Pascal, *Pensees* (London: Penguin Books, 1995), 45.

2. St. Augustine, *Confessions* (New York: Oxford University Press, 1991),

3. Alfred Edersheim, *The Life and Times of Jesus the Messiah*, vol. 2 (New York: Longmans, Green, and Co., 1896), 275.

4. Pascal, *Pensees*, 127.

| 11 | Coming Out

1. Our English idiom says we "believe in Christ." In Greek that would be *pistis ein* (in) *Christos*. But the idiomatic phrase in the Greek New Testament is *pistis eis* (into) *Christos*. We don't believe *in* Christ, we believe *into* him. This helps me understand Paul's recurring phrase that to be "saved" is to be "in Christ." How is one *in* Christ unless he or she has been brought *into* Christ? This is done by faith—believing into. The "into" becomes mutual. Jesus prayed to the Father, "...just as you are in me and I am in you. May they also be in us ... I in them and you in me." (Jn 17.21-23)

| 12 | Surprised Again

1. Adelaide A. Pollard, "Have Thine Own Way, Lord," (Public Domain, 1907).

2. Lewis, *Surprised By Joy, 229.*

| Epilogue | Happy, Joyous, and Free

1. John Newton, "Amazing Grace," (Public Domain, 1800).

2. Anonymous, *Alcoholics Anonymous*, 2nd ed., *164.*

3. Lewis, *Surprised By Joy*, 217. In *Space Time and Deity* Alexander differentiates between "enjoyment" and "contemplation." C. S. Lewis comments: "These are technical terms in Alexander's philosophy; 'Enjoyment' has nothing to do with pleasure, nor 'Contemplation' with the contemplative life. When you see a table, you 'enjoy' the act of seeing and 'contemplate' the table."

4. Lewis, *Surprised By Joy*, 119.

5. "Something's Coming," in *West Side Story*. Music: Leonard Bernstein. Lyric: Stephen Sondheim. (1957).

6. See Jürgen Moltmann, *Theology of Hope: On the Ground and the Implications of a Christian Eschatology* (New York: Harper & Row, 1967).

7. T. S. Eliot, "The Hollow Men," in *Selected Poems* (Harmondsworth, Middlesex, UK: Penguin Books, 1948), Stanza V, lines 30-31.

8. Anonymous, *Alcoholics Anonymous*, 2nd ed., *59*.

9. I fear that Bible expositors will shudder at the conjoining of Johannine and Pauline texts in this manner. But while the conjoining may do violence to the letter, I think it preserves the spirit of the texts.

10. Helen Keller, BrainyQuotes.com http://www.brainyquote.com/quotes/quotes/h/helenkelle101301.html (accessed October 22 2011).

11. William James, *The Varieties of Religious Experience* (New York: Classic Books International, 2010), 69. James attributes the concept of contrasting once-born and twice-born personalities to the writings of Francis W. Newman.

∞

| Works Cited |

Anonymous. *Alcoholics Anonymous: The Story of How Many Thousands of Men and Women Have Recovered from Alcoholism.* 2nd ed. New York: Alcoholics Anonymous World Services, 1955.

Anonymous. *Alcoholics Anonymous: The Story of How Many Thousands of Men and Women Have Recovered from Alcoholism.* 4th ed. New York: Alcoholics Anonymous World Services, 2001.

Anonymous. *Twelve Steps and Twelve Traditions.* New York: Alcoholics Anonymous Publishing, 1953.

Anonymous. *Twenty-Four Hours a Day.* Revised ed. City Center: Hazelden Foundation, 1975.

Augustine, St. *Confessions.* New York: Oxford University Press, 1991.

Bernstein, Leonard, and Stephen Sondheim. "Something's Coming," in *West Side Story,* 1957.

Bock, Jerry, and Sheldon Hamick. "Do You Love Me?," in *Fiddler on the Roof,* 1964.

Boyd, Gregory. *The Myth of a Christian Religion.* Grand Rapids: Zondervan, 2009.

Brooks, Clara M. "What a Mighty God We Serve!" Public Domain, 1907.

Durrell, Lawrence. *Balthazar: A Novel.* New York: Dutton, 1958.

Edersheim, Alfred. *The Life and Times of Jesus the Messiah*. Vol. 2. 2 vols. 8th, rev. ed. New York: Longmans, Green, and Co., 1896.

Eliot, T. S. "The Hollow Men." In *Selected Poems*, Harmondsworth, Middlesex, UK: Penguin Books, 1948.

Gibran, Kahil. "The Madman." In *Spiritual World*. Guildford, UK: White Crow Books, 2009.

Ginsberg, Allen. *Howl, and Other Poems*. The Pocket Poets Series, No. 4. San Francisco: City Lights Pocket Bookshop, 1956.

Grinnan, Edward, "My Faith: How Storytelling Saved My Life," CNN http://religion.blogs.cnn.com/2011/08/07/my-faith-how-storytelling-saved-my-life/?hpt=hp_c2 (accessed August 11 2011).

Henderson, Jim, Todd Hunter, and Greg Spinks. *The Outsider Interviews*. Grand Rapids: Baker Books, 2010.

James, William. *The Varieties of Religious Experience*. New York: Classic Books International, 2010.

Keller, Helen, BrainyQuotes.com http://www.brainyquote.com/quotes/quotes/h/helenkelle101301.html (accessed October 22 2011).

Lewis, C. S. *Surprised By Joy: The Shape of My Early Life*. Orlando: Harcourt Brace & Company, 1955.

MacDonald, George. *Unspoken Sermons, Vol. 1, 2, & 3*. Centenary ed. The Sunrise Centenary Editions of the Works of George Macdonald Sermons. Eureka: Sunrise Books Publishers, 2004.

Moltmann, Jürgen. *Theology of Hope: On the Ground and the Implications of a Christian Eschatology*. New York: Harper & Row, 1967.

Newton, John. "Amazing Grace." 1800. Public Domain.

Pascal, Blaise. *Pensees*. London: Penguin Books, 1995.

Peck, M. Scott. *People of the Lie: The Hope for Healing Human Evil*. New York: Simon and Schuster, 1983.

Phillips, J.B., *Your God Is Too Small*. New York: Macmillan, 1953.

Pinsky, D. Drew, "Allow Weiner to Save His Marriage," CNN Opinion http://www.cnn.com/2011/OPINION/06/07/drew.pinsky.weiner/index.html?hpt=hp_bn9 (accessed June 7 2011).

Pollard, Adelaide A. *Have Thine Own Way, Lord*. Public Domain, 1907.

Santayana, George. *The Life of Reason*. Vol. 1: Reason in Common Sense. New York: Scribner's, 1905.

Shakespeare, William, "Hamlet," http://shakespeare.mit.edu/ http://shakespeare.mit.edu/hamlet/full.html (accessed October 23 2011).

Sill, Edward Rowland. "An Adage from the Orient." In *Poetical Works*. New York: Houghton, Mifflin, 1906.

Springsteen, Bruce. "Hungry Heart." ASCAP, 1980.

Thompson, Earl. A Garden of Sand. New York: Carroll & Graf, 2001.

Twain, Mark (Samuel Clemens). *The Adventures of Tom Sawyer*. Colorado Springs: Picadilly Books, 2010.

∞

If you liked *Prisoner of Hope*,

get your copy of Ed's first book:

"Just a thought…" –e. Manna for the Mind

Thoughts about *"Just a thought…" –e. : Manna for the Mind*

This thought-provoking book offers short readings on a wide variety of topics prompted by Dr. Ed Cook's engagement with culture and the Christian faith. In the age of sound bites and instant gratification, we sometimes forget that elements of our life deserve more consideration than can be expressed in tweets, posts, and Facebook status updates. The chapters are short, the writing is pithy, and the pages will prompt readers to develop and contemplate their own questions regarding this brave new world in which we find ourselves at the start of the twenty-first century. Just as in life, the joy is often in the journey rather than the destination. The richness of this reading experience may often be found in the questions contemplated rather than in answers discovered. So read, enjoy, and think a bit. You may not agree with everything presented but remember, no offense is intended because, after all, what's offered is just a thought.

To order a personally inscribed copy of *"Just a thought…" –e.*

1. Go to www.justathought-e.com
2. Click on "Buy the Book" in the menu bar
3. Click on "Buy Now" at the bottom of the page

Also available at www.harmonpress.com & www.amazon.com

CPSIA information can be obtained
at www.ICGtesting.com
Printed in the USA
BVHW061550070222
628203BV00001B/189